Congressional
Research
Service

Federal Programs Related to Indoor Pollution by Chemicals

Linda-Jo Schierow
Specialist in Environmental Policy

David M. Bearden
Specialist in Environmental Policy

July 23, 2012

Congressional Research Service

7-5700

www.crs.gov

R42620

Summary

"Toxic" drywall, formaldehyde emissions, mold, asbestos, lead-based paint, radon, PCBs in caulk, and many other indoor pollution problems have concerned federal policy makers and regulators during the last 30 years. Some problems have been resolved, others remain of concern, and new indoor pollution problems continually emerge. This report describes common indoor pollutants and health effects that have been linked to indoor pollution, federal statutes that have been used to address indoor pollution, key issues, and some general policy options for Congress.

Indoor pollutants are chemicals that are potentially harmful to people and found in the habitable portions of buildings, including homes, schools, offices, factories, and other public gathering places. Some indoor pollutants, like lead or ozone, are also outdoor pollutants. Others, like formaldehyde or asbestos, are primarily indoor pollutants. Indoor pollutants may be natural (for example, carbon monoxide or radon) or synthetic (polychlorinated biphenyls [PCBs]), and may originate indoors or outdoors. They may be deliberately produced, naturally occurring, or inadvertent byproducts of human activities. For example, they may arise indoors as uncontrolled emissions from building materials, paints, or furnishings, from evaporation following the use of cleaning supplies or pesticides, or as a combustion byproduct as a result of heating or cooking. Some pollution that originates outdoors infiltrates through porous basements (e.g., radon) or is inadvertently brought into indoor spaces, perhaps through heating or air conditioning systems or in contaminated drinking water. Often pollutants accumulate indoors as a result of deliberate improvements to increase energy efficiency, for example by reducing building permeability to air.

The health risks posed by indoor pollutants have concerned scientists for many years. Because people spend a high percentage of their time indoors, and concentrations of pollutants often are higher in indoor air than outdoor air, the risks due to exposure can be higher than many other environmental risks. Moreover, a 2011 report by the Institute of Medicine warns that many indoor environmental quality problems might get worse if adaptations to climate change are made without better information and programs aimed at pollution prevention.

No federal agency has broad authority concerning pollution indoors. Nonetheless, numerous federal agencies have some authority to control particular indoor pollutants or sources of pollution or the quality of indoor environments in a particular class of structures. For example, the U.S. Environmental Protection Agency (EPA) has authority under the Toxic Substances Control Act (TSCA) to study and issue safety guidelines for radon and lead-based paint hazards. The Comprehensive Environmental Response, Compensation, and Liability Act (CERCLA) authorizes EPA also to respond to releases of hazardous substances into the outdoor environment which may migrate indoors. The Consumer Product Safety Commission (CPSC) has authority to set emission limits for, and to restrict uses of, certain chemicals in consumer products. The Department of Housing and Urban Development (HUD) and the General Services Administration (GSA) regulate some indoor pollutants in federal buildings. These and other agencies have conducted research to examine the risks of various indoor pollutants.

Concerns about coordination of federal efforts to address indoor pollution have been expressed by the general public, the U.S. Government Accountability Office (GAO), and the U.S. Congress. But any federal response to indoor pollution is complicated by the need to coordinate with local and state governments as well to address potentially overlapping jurisdictions and resources. Options for Congress range from maintenance or improvement of the status quo to reduction or expansion of federal involvement in research, information dissemination, or regulation.

Contents

Contacts

Introduction

"Toxic" drywall, formaldehyde emissions, mold, asbestos, lead-based paint, radon, PCBs in caulk, and many other indoor pollution problems have concerned scientists, federal policy makers, and regulators during the last 30 years. Some problems have been resolved, others remain of concern, and new indoor pollution problems continually emerge, often unexpectedly.

Because people spend a high percentage of their time indoors, and concentrations of pollutants often are higher in indoor air than outdoors, the human health risks indoors generally can be greater relative to risks from exposure to pollutants in the ambient (i.e., outdoor) air.[1] In 1987, indoor air quality was identified by EPA scientists as one of the greatest sources of environmental risk to human health.[2] EPA's Science Advisory Board, an independent body of experts, reviewed and endorsed this comparative risk ranking and in 1990 called upon the agency to give a higher priority to funding such high-risk environmental problems.[3] In 1997, the Presidential and Congressional Commission on Risk Assessment and Risk Management again considered the relative risks presented by various environmental problems and concluded that indoor pollution could pose a substantial public health risk.[4] In 2011, a report by the Institute of Medicine warned that many indoor air quality problems might get worse if adaptations to climate change are made without better information and programs aimed at pollution prevention.[5] For example, methods to make homes better insulated and more energy efficient may result in less circulation with outdoor air, potentially increasing indoor concentrations of pollutants unless effective filtration or treatment technologies can be incorporated.

This report describes common indoor pollutants, discusses federal statutes that have been used to address indoor pollution, and analyzes key issues surrounding some general policy options for federal policy makers. The focus is on indoor chemical contaminants, rather than on temperature, humidity, or pollution from animals, fungal or bacterial organisms, or plant pests.[6]

Indoor Pollutants and Health Concerns

Indoor pollutants are chemicals that are potentially harmful to people and may be found in the habitable portions of buildings, including homes, schools, offices, factories, and other public gathering places. Indoor pollutants are many and varied. Many exposures may be through indoor

---

[1] Committee on the Effect of Climate Change on Indoor Air Quality and Public Health, Institute of Medicine, *Climate Change, the Indoor Environment, and Health*, prepublication copy, National Academy Press, p. 1-1, http://www.nap.edu/catalog.php?record_id=13115.

[2] U.S. EPA, Office of Policy Analysis. Unfinished Business: A Comparative Assessment of Environmental Problems. Washington, U.S. Environmental Protection Agency, February 1987. p. XIII.

[3] EPA Science Advisory Board, Reducing Risk: Setting Priorities and Strategies for Environmental Protection (September 1990).

[4] The Presidential and Congressional Commission on Risk Assessment and Risk Management, Risk Assessment and Risk Management in Regulatory Decision-Making, 2 Vols. (January 29, 1997).

[5] Ibid.

[6] Mold toxins are not discussed in this report, although, like pollen, they may be considered indoor air pollutants. Because they are naturally occurring and of biological origin, federal agencies do not generally attempt to control them through regulation. Several agencies, such as EPA and CDC, do conduct research on occurrence, cause, and potential health effects of these contaminants and provide information about them to the public on the internet.

air. Some substances, like lead or ozone, are also ambient (outdoor) air pollutants. Others, like formaldehyde or asbestos, may be found either indoors or out, but are most often of concern when found at unhealthful concentrations indoors. Indoor pollutants may be natural (for example, carbon monoxide or radon) or synthetic (such as polychlorinated biphenyls [PCBs]), may originate indoors or outdoors, and may be deliberately produced, naturally occurring, or inadvertent byproducts of human activities. People may be exposed to indoor contaminants in the air, tap water, or dust by inhalation, skin contact, or mouth.

Some examples of common indoor pollutants are discussed below.

Combustion Byproducts

Some indoor pollution originates indoors as a result of fuel combustion for home heating or cooking.[7] Fuel type, combustion efficiency, and ventilation affect the nature and extent of pollutant emissions and accumulations. Pollutants produced by combustion include smoke and carbon monoxide.

Smoke contains a number of potentially harmful gases and small particles which may aggravate asthma and other health conditions.[8] In developing countries, indoor smoke is a major concern. According to the World Health Organization (WHO), "[i]ndoor air pollution generated largely by inefficient and poorly ventilated stoves burning biomass fuels such as wood, crop waste and dung, or coal—is responsible for the deaths of an estimated 2 million people annually."[9]

Indoor combustion also is a concern in the United States, especially in homes without adequate furnaces where people may rely upon unvented space heaters or other devices to keep warm. Indoor combustion also is particularly common in the United States during emergencies when electricity or vented equipment may become unavailable, prompting residents to run generators indoors or to heat or cook with unvented portable devices such as barbeque grills. Accumulation of carbon monoxide, which is a colorless and odorless gas, is responsible for numerous deaths annually in the United States.[10]

Smoking that produces environmental tobacco smoke is another source of indoor air pollution. The respiratory tracts of young children are especially vulnerable to infections as a result of exposure to secondhand smoke.[11]

---

[7] EPA, "An Introduction to Indoor Air Quality: Carbon Monoxide," http://www.epa.gov/iaq/co.html.

[8] EPA, Region 10: the Pacific Northwest, "Health Effects of Fine Particles and Smoke," http://yosemite.epa.gov/R10/AIRPAGE.NSF/webpage/Health+Effects+of+Fine+Particles+and+Smoke.

[9] WHO, "Global Health Risks: Mortality and Burden of Disease Attributable to Selected Major Risks," WHO, Geneva, 2009, http://www.who.int/healthinfo/global_burden_disease/GlobalHealthRisks_report_Front.pdf. http://www.who.int/heli/risks/indoorair/indoorair/en/index.html.

[10] According to the Consumer Product Safety Commission, on average 184 deaths occurred accidentally due to carbon monoxide poisoning 2004-2007. Matthew V. Hnatov, 2011, *Non-Fire Carbon Monoxide Deaths Associated with the Use of Consumer Products*, 2007 Annual Estimates, http://www.cpsc.gov/library/foia/foia11/os/co10.pdf.

[11] EPA, "Health Effects of Exposure to Secondhand Smoke," October 3, 2010, http://www.epa.gov/smokefree/healtheffects.html.

Radon Gas

Radon is a naturally occurring, extremely toxic, colorless gas that is formed naturally from rocks and soil as a result of radioactive decay of radium. Radon emissions vary widely, but high levels of radon contamination occur in every state. Radon gas can enter homes through porous basement walls or dissolved in drinking water from which it may escape into the air, for example, during showering.[12] Indoors, radon gas may accumulate to dangerous levels. EPA recommends that every home be tested for radon levels.[13] According to EPA, exposure to radon in homes accounts for about 20,000 lung cancer deaths annually.[14]

Asbestos

Asbestos is a fibrous mineral that is found in certain natural rock formations.[15] It was mined and widely used in the manufacture of fire-retardant materials, including automotive brake linings, roof, ceiling, and floor tiles, and insulation for furnaces, air ducts, and pipes.[16] As the asbestos materials in buildings have deteriorated over time, and when they have been removed for remodeling or otherwise disturbed, asbestos fibers have been released to indoor air. When inhaled, such asbestos fibers have caused lung cancer and other lung diseases.[17]

Lead

Lead hazards are found in many homes and other buildings where lead-based paint has been applied and is deteriorating, lead solder or plumbing contaminates drinking water, or contaminated soil is tracked indoors. Childhood exposure to lead hazards can lead to brain and nervous system damage, behavior and learning problems, slowed growth, hearing problems, and headaches, according to EPA.[18] Although exposure most commonly is to the lead in dust that gets onto hands and then enters a body through the mouth, indoor air inhalation of lead also can occur, for example, as a result of home renovation, or when contaminated outdoor air enters buildings.[19]

Formaldehyde, PCBs, and other Industrial Chemicals

Sometimes synthetic chemicals accumulate to noxious levels in indoor air or dust as a result of uncontrolled emissions from building materials, paints, or furnishings, or evaporation following the use of cleaning supplies.[20] Other synthetic chemicals may be inadvertently released (e.g., an

---

[12] EPA, "Radon," August 12, 2011, http://www.epa.gov/radiation/radionuclides/radon.html#contact.

[13] EPA, "What Is Radon?" October 14, 2010, http://iaq.supportportal.com/ics/support/kbAnswer.asp?deptID=23007&task=knowledge&questionID=22510.

[14] EPA, "Living Healthy and Green Starts from the Ground Up," August 8, 2011, http://www.epa.gov/radon/index.html.

[15] EPA, "Naturally Occurring Asbestos," June 7, 2010, http://www.epa.gov/asbestos/pubs/clean.html.

[16] EPA, "Asbestos," April 18, 2011, http://www.epa.gov/asbestos/.

[17] Ibid.

[18] EPA, "Lead in Paint, Dust, and Soil: Basic Information," August 16, 2011, http://www.epa.gov/lead/pubs/leadinfo.htm#health.

[19] Ibid.

[20] John D. Spengler, "Overview," In: *Report of the Surgeon General's Workshop on Healthy Indoor Environment*, (continued...)

---

ozone-producing machine may be used to "freshen" air). Still other indoor pollution originates outdoors but intrudes into homes, for example as contaminated air infiltrates through porous basement walls or is brought into the home through heating or air conditioning systems, or as contaminated drinking water. Outdoor contamination which migrates into the indoor air through groundwater and soil beneath homes and buildings often is referred to as "vapor intrusion."

Prominent examples of industrial pollutants that have been found indoors include formaldehyde, which is emitted to air from some composite wood products; PCBs released from deteriorating caulk, paints, coatings, or plastics; and contamination from dry cleaning solvents, such as trichloroethylene (TCE) or perchloroethylene (PERC), which have migrated indoors through vapor intrusion at many sites. There also has been increasing attention to the potential risks of indoor exposure to perchlorate contamination through vapor intrusion or groundwater sources used for drinking water supplies. Perchlorate is a substance commonly used in solid propellants in military munitions and commercial fireworks.

Pesticides

Pesticides released within buildings or around the foundation of buildings also may be indoor contaminants. Termiticides, insecticides, flea foggers, and roach or rodent control products are particularly common sources of toxic chemicals indoors. Even years after use, some of these products may persist where sunlight and rain cannot reach them. For example, scientists found relatively high levels of DDT in indoor dust samples taken in Cape Cod recently.[21]

Federal Authorities and Programs

No federal agency has broad statutory authority concerning pollution indoors. On the other hand, numerous federal agencies (at least 23 in spring 2012) have some authority to conduct research or to control particular indoor pollutants, sources of pollution, or environmental quality in particular structures. For example, the EPA has some authority under the Toxic Substances Control Act (TSCA) to address asbestos in schools; building standards, testing, and research related to radon; and lead-based paint hazards in housing. Key agencies and authorizing statutes are briefly described below. For more information about the authorities and activities of federal agencies with respect to indoor air quality, see EPA's 1989 Report to Congress on Indoor Air Quality, Volume 2, chapter 8.[22] For additional background information about the research conducted by federal agencies, see the 1999 report by the U.S. General Accounting Office (GAO, now the Government Accountability Office), *Indoor Pollution: Status of Federal Research Activities*, GAO-RCED-99-254.[23] A more recent summary of federal research and development and outreach activities related to indoor environments is available in *Report of the Surgeon General's Workshop on Healthy Indoor Environment*, January 12-13, 2005.[24] Information is also available

---

(...continued)

January 2005, Department of Health and Human Services, p. 4-5.

[21] Ibid.

[22] EPA, "Report to Congress on Indoor Air Quality: Volume II - Assessment and Control of Indoor Air Pollution, 1989," EPA/400/1-89/001C. Hereafter EPA Report to Congress, Vol. II.

[23] GAO, "Indoor Pollution: Status of Federal Research Activities," GAO-RCED-99-254.

[24] National Institutes of Health, Bethesda, MD, HHS, http://www.ncbi.nlm.nih.gov/books/NBK44638/, visited July 19, (continued...)

on agency websites. For direct links to some agencies' indoor environmental quality programs, visit http://www.epa.gov/iaq/ciaq/members html.

Environmental Protection Agency

The origin of the Environmental Protection Agency (EPA) is rooted in a reorganization of the executive branch under the Nixon Administration. In Reorganization Plan No. 3 of 1970, President Nixon proposed the establishment of EPA to integrate the administration of numerous federal pollution control laws that had been carried out by several federal agencies.[25] This plan was part of a broader effort to reorganize an array of environmental responsibilities of many federal agencies. The Nixon Administration created EPA through this reorganization with congressional approval under procedures established in the Reorganization Act of 1949, as amended.[26] This reorganization provided the administrative framework for the creation of EPA. However, numerous federal environmental laws actually provide the statutory authority for the agency to carry out its overall mission to protect human health and the environment, with each law authorizing specific responsibilities. EPA's responsibilities generally have grown over time as Congress has amended these laws and enacted new laws to address particular needs. EPA has delegated the day-to-day implementation of many of these laws to the states, as provided in the state delegation authorities of the requisite statutes.

EPA has used its various statutory authorities to address indoor pollution in numerous ways over time. Some of EPA's authorizing statutes also have given the agency specific authority to characterize indoor air problems; identify, assess, and implement strategies to mitigate hazards; and disseminate information about indoor environmental quality control.[27] Selected noteworthy statutory authorities and mandates related to indoor pollution are abstracted below.[28]

Toxic Substances Control Act (15 U.S.C. 2601 et seq.)

Title I, General Authorities over Toxic Substances

Title I of the Toxic Substances Control Act (TSCA) provides very broad authority to EPA to identify and control the manufacture, distribution, and use of chemicals. This authority extends to chemicals that may be indoor pollutants, with the exception that TSCA does not cover chemicals regulated under other laws, such as pesticides, tobacco, nuclear material, substances subject to

---

(...continued)

2012.

[25] Reorganization Plan No. 3 of 1970, and President Nixon's accompanying message submitting the plan to Congress, are available on EPA's website: http://www.epa.gov/aboutepa/history/org/origins/reorg.html. Section 2 of the plan identified the individual programs and activities of federal agencies transferred to EPA. The full text of Reorganization Plan No. 3 of 1970 also is codified in the note to 42 U.S.C. §4321. This provision is the "Congressional declaration and purpose" of the National Environmental Policy Act (NEPA). Although Reorganization Plan No. 3 is codified in the note to this provision, the plan was not included in NEPA itself, and NEPA did not create EPA.

[26] 5 U.S.C. §901 et seq.

[27] EPA Report to Congress, Vol. II, p. 9-1.

[28] For more information about the general statutory authorities of the federal environmental laws which EPA administers, see CRS Report RL30798, *Environmental Laws Summaries of Major Statutes Administered by the Environmental Protection Agency.*

---

certain taxes (e.g., alcohol), and food, drugs, cosmetics, and devices regulated under the Federal Food, Drug, and Cosmetic Act.

TSCA authorizes EPA to require manufacturers to test a chemical for toxicity, and the law directs EPA to control exposure to any chemical that poses an unreasonable risk to health or the environment. However, before controlling risks, EPA "must weigh the reduction in risk attributable to the regulation against the regulatory burdens to society, including costs. Further, EPA must use the 'least burdensome' sanction, taking into account whether the health threat could be eliminated or reduced to a sufficient extent under other Federal statutes."[29]

Among the eight chemical substances that ever have been restricted under the general authority of TSCA Title I (40 CFR Part 260) is the indoor pollutant asbestos, for which EPA banned all applications that were not already in use.[30] In addition, TSCA 6(e) explicitly requires EPA regulation of polychlorinated biphenyls (PCBs). Under other TSCA authorities, EPA has gathered data or restricted new uses for thousands of other new and existing chemicals, some of which are actual or potential indoor pollutants.

Title II, Asbestos Hazard Emergency Response Act (AHERA)

Congress enacted Title II of TSCA, the Asbestos Hazard Emergency Response Act (AHERA), to address asbestos hazards in schools. The law requires EPA to set standards for responding to the presence of asbestos in schools. The standards, set at levels adequate to protect public health and the environment, identify appropriate response actions that depend on the physical condition of asbestos. Schools, in turn, are required to inspect for asbestos-containing material, and to develop and implement a plan for managing any such material.

Title II requires asbestos contractors and analytical laboratories to be certified, and schools to use certified persons for abatement work. Training and accreditation requirements also apply to inspectors, contractors, and workers performing asbestos abatement work in all public and commercial buildings. Other Title II requirements (such as mandates that buildings be inspected for asbestos) have not been extended to non-school buildings.

To enforce requirements, TSCA Title II authorizes EPA to take emergency action with respect to schools if school officials do not act to protect children. The act also authorizes citizen action with respect to asbestos-containing material in a school and to compel action by EPA, either through administrative petition or judicial action. Civil penalties are authorized for violations, such as failing to conduct an inspection or to develop a school management plan.

Concern about how schools would pay for required actions was addressed in separate legislation (the Asbestos School Hazard Abatement Act of 1984, or ASHAA, P.L. 98-377). It established a program offering grants and interest-free loans to schools with serious asbestos problems and demonstrated financial need. Repaid ASHAA loans are returned to an Asbestos Trust Fund to become a dedicated source of revenues for future asbestos control projects.

---

[29] EPA Report to Congress, Vol. II, p. 8-5.

[30] The other seven chemicals are certain chlorofluoroalkanes (now regulated under the Clean Air Act), polychlorinated biphenyls (PCBs), elemental mercury, lead-based paint, metalworking fluids, hexavalent chromium use to treat water in comfort cooling towers, and dioxin (later regulated under the authority of the Clean Water Act and the Resource Conservation and Recovery Act). Current regulations may be found at 40 CFR 763.160-179.

Title III, Indoor Radon Abatement

In 1988, Congress added to TSCA a third title, Indoor Radon Abatement (15 U.S.C. 2661 et seq., P.L. 100-551), to provide financial and technical assistance to states that choose to support radon monitoring and control; neither monitoring nor abatement of radon is required by the act. Title III requires EPA to update its pamphlet "A Citizen's Guide to Radon," to develop model construction standards and techniques for controlling radon levels within new buildings, and to provide technical assistance to states. EPA is to provide technical assistance by: establishing an information clearinghouse; publishing public information materials; establishing a national database of radon levels detected, organized by state; providing information to professional organizations representing private firms involved in building design and construction; submitting to Congress a plan for providing financial and technical assistance to states; operating cooperative projects with states; conducting research to develop, test, and evaluate radon measurement methods and protocols; developing and demonstrating new methods of radon measurement and mitigation, including methods that are suitable for use in nonresidential child care facilities; operating a voluntary program to rate radon measurement and mitigation devices and methods and the effectiveness of private firms and individuals offering radon-related services; and designing and implementing training seminars. In 1994, EPA promulgated final standards for the control of radon in new residential buildings.[31]

The proficiency rating program and certification for training programs collect fees for service, and therefore are meant to be self-supporting, but Congress authorized $1.5 million to be appropriated to establish these programs. A matching grant program was established for the purpose of assisting states in developing and implementing programs for radon assessment and mitigation, with funds targeted to states or projects that made efforts to ensure adoption of EPA's model construction standards and techniques for new buildings; gave preference to low-income persons; or addressed serious and extensive radon contamination problems or had the potential to reduce risk or to develop innovative assessment techniques, mitigation measures, or management approaches.

Other sections of Title III require EPA to: conduct a study to determine the extent of radon contamination in schools; identify and list areas of the United States with a high probability of having high levels of indoor radon; make grants or cooperative agreements to establish and operate at least three regional radon training centers; and provide guidance to federal agencies on radon measurement, risk assessment, and remedial measures.

Title IV, Lead Exposure Reduction

The 102nd Congress added Title IV to TSCA when it enacted the Residential Lead-Based Paint Hazard Reduction Act of 1992 as Title X in the Housing and Community Development Act of 1992 (P.L. 102-550). TSCA Title IV directs EPA to ensure that

- people engaged in detection and control of lead hazards are properly trained and contractors are certified;

- the public is informed about lead hazards; and

---

[31] 59 *Federal Register* 13402, March 21, 1994.

- there are quality controls for laboratories, laboratory methods, and commercial products used to detect or reduce risks associated with lead-based paint.

Title IV explicitly applies these requirements to federal facilities and federal activities (including federally-funded activities) that may create a lead hazard. In addition, Congress directed EPA to promulgate guidelines for the renovation and remodeling of buildings or other structures when these activities might create a hazard.

Title IV authorizes states to propose programs to train and certify inspectors and contractors engaged in the detection or control of lead-based paint hazards. States also may develop the required informational pamphlets. TSCA requires EPA to promulgate a model state program that may be adopted by any state. Congress gave EPA the authority to approve or disapprove authorization for state proposals and to provide grants for states to develop and implement authorized programs. A federal program must be established, administered, and enforced by EPA in each state without an authorized program.

Title V, Reducing Risks in Schools

At the end of 2007, the 110th Congress added a fifth title to TSCA, subtitled Healthy High-Performance Schools. Enacted as Title IV, Subtitle E (section 461) of P.L. 110-140, the Energy Independence and Security Act of 2007, TSCA Title V authorizes EPA to establish a state grant program to provide technical assistance for EPA programs to schools and develop and implement state school environmental health programs. State programs must include standards for school building design, construction, and renovation, and identify ongoing school building environmental problems and recommended solutions. Environmental problems specifically mentioned in the law include "contaminants, hazardous substances, and pollutant emissions." EPA's authority to provide grants expires five years after the date of enactment.

Title V requires the EPA Administrator, in consultation with the Secretary of Education and the Secretary of Health and Human Services, to issue voluntary guidelines for selecting sites for schools (presumably new schools), and voluntary guidelines for developing and implementing state environmental health programs for schools. These guidelines must take into account "environmental problems, contaminants, hazardous substances, and pollutant emissions"; natural day lighting; ventilation; heating and cooling; moisture control and mold; maintenance, cleaning, and pest control; acoustics; and "other issues relating to the health, comfort, productivity, and performance of occupants of the school facilities." In addition, Title V requires that the guidelines provide "technical assistance on siting, design, management, and operation of school facilities"; collaborate with children's environmental health centers in school environmental investigations; assist states and the public to better understand and improve the environmental health of children; and take into account "the special vulnerability of children in low-income and minority communities to exposures from contaminants, hazardous substances, and pollutant emissions."

Title VI, Limiting Formaldehyde Emissions

In July 2010, Congress enacted the Formaldehyde Standards for Composite Wood Products Act (P.L. 111-199), adding a new Title VI to TSCA. The new title mandates specific formaldehyde emission standards for hardwood plywood, medium-density fiberboard, and particleboard that is sold, supplied, offered for sale, or manufactured in the United States. The standards are based on the voluntary national formaldehyde emissions standards established by ASTM International (formerly known as the American Society for Testing and Materials), method ASTM E-1333-96 (2002).

EPA is required to promulgate regulations ensuring compliance with the emission standards and must include provisions relating to labeling, chain of custody requirements, sell-through provisions; ultra low-emitting formaldehyde resins, finished goods, third-party testing and certification; auditing and reporting of third-party certifiers; recordkeeping; enforcement, laminated products; and exceptions for products and components containing "de minimis amounts" of composite wood products. The new law prohibits stockpiling of products manufactured before the effective date of the act for sale after that date. Also prohibited is any requirement for labeling products manufactured prior to the "designated date of manufacture."

Comprehensive Environmental Response, Compensation, and Liability Act (42 U.S.C. 9601 et seq.)

The Comprehensive Environmental Response, Compensation, and Liability Act is the primary federal statute that authorizes EPA to respond to releases of hazardous substances into the environment.[32] CERCLA established the Hazardous Substance Superfund Trust Fund to finance appropriations for EPA to carry out the authorities of the statute under the Superfund program.[33] The program primarily focuses on the cleanup of the most hazardous sites which EPA has placed on the National Priorities List (NPL).[34] The states also participate in cleanup decisions at these sites, and may share a portion of the cleanup costs if the responsible parties cannot be found or cannot pay to satisfy their liability.[35] EPA oversees the cleanup of federal facilities under the Superfund program in conjunction with the states, but the agencies which administer those facilities are responsible for performing the cleanup with their own appropriations. Most contaminated federal facilities served national defense purposes and are administered by the Department of Defense and the Department of Energy, discussed later in this report.

For the purposes of CERCLA, the term "environment" is defined in the statute to encompass only the outdoor environment (i.e., ambient air, land surface or subsurface strata, surface water, or groundwater, including drinking water supplies).[36] Although CERCLA principally applies to releases into the outdoor environment, EPA's policy is to apply CERCLA to a release inside a home or a building if the release originated from an outside source and subsequently migrated indoors presenting an exposure risk.[37] Otherwise, CERCLA generally prohibits EPA from using

---

[32] For a more in-depth examination of the authorities of CERCLA, see CRS Report R41039, *Comprehensive Environmental Response, Compensation, and Liability Act A Summary of Superfund Cleanup Authorities and Related Provisions of the Act*, by David M. Bearden.

[33] See the "Hazardous Substance Superfund Trust Fund" section in CRS Report R41039, *Comprehensive Environmental Response, Compensation, and Liability Act A Summary of Superfund Cleanup Authorities and Related Provisions of the Act*, by David M. Bearden.

[34] EPA also may perform more limited "removal" actions at sites not listed on the NPL to address immediate hazards.

[35] As a condition for the obligation of federal Superfund appropriations, states generally must agree to pay 10% of the costs of constructing cleanup remedies, and 100% of the costs of operating and maintaining them over the long-term. There is no state cost-share requirement for Superfund emergency removal actions, only long-term remedial actions.

[36] 42 U.S.C. §9601(8).

[37] EPA, Office of Solid Waste and Emergency Response, OSWER Directive 9360.3-12, August 12, 1993, *Response Actions at Sites with Contamination Inside Buildings*. The directive is available on EPA's Superfund program website: http://www.epa.gov/superfund/policy/remedy/pdfs/93-60312-s.pdf.

---

the authorities of the statute to respond to releases originating from, and remaining contained within, a home or building, unless there is the potential for an indoor release to migrate outdoors and therefore constitute a release into the environment as defined in the statute.

Section 104(a)(3) of CERCLA explicitly limits EPA's authority to respond to releases of naturally occurring substances (either indoors or outdoors), and to releases from structural components within a home or building if the release would result solely in indoor exposures.[38] However, Section 104(a)(4) provides an exception if EPA determines that the hazard constitutes a public health emergency, and no other person with the authority and capability to respond to the emergency will do so in a timely manner.[39] To date, EPA has made a public health emergency declaration under CERCLA at one site, the Libby Asbestos Site in Montana. EPA Administrator Lisa Jackson issued the declaration for this site on June 17, 2009, because of potential risks in homes and buildings contaminated with vermiculite, a form of asbestos, which originated from the Libby mine.[40] As such, the Libby Asbestos Site is somewhat unique. In practice, CERCLA most frequently has been used to respond to indoor pollution resulting from contaminated water supplies or vapor intrusion from external sources of contamination.

As noted in the section on "Indoor Pollutants and Health Concerns," vapor intrusion may occur when contaminants in groundwater or soil beneath a home or building may migrate into a structure and be released into indoor air. For example, contaminants may be released indoors if they migrate upward from groundwater through the soil column and penetrate porous basement floors and walls, or cracks in foundations. As the potential health risks from vapor intrusion have received increasing attention, EPA has been considering whether to include a ranking criteria for these risks in determining the eligibility of sites for listing on the NPL.[41] Historically, there have been no listing criteria for vapor intrusion.

Sites at which vapor intrusion is the only pathway of exposure generally have not been listed on the NPL, making them ineligible for Superfund appropriations to pay for the long-term remediation (as only sites listed on the NPL are eligible).[42] This limitation does not apply to NPL sites at which the responsible parties pay for the cleanup, and the sites therefore do not rely on Superfund appropriations (including federal facilities). EPA still may use Superfund appropriations to perform more limited emergency removal actions to respond to vapor intrusion (or other risks), regardless of whether a site is listed on the NPL.[43] While the consideration of NPL listing criteria has been under way, EPA also has been revising its 2002 policy on evaluating risks from vapor intrusion at sites that are eligible under the Superfund program.[44] This guidance also applies to performing site assessments under CERCLA at "brownfields" not addressed under

---

[38] 42 U.S.C. §9604(a)(3).

[39] 42 U.S.C. §9604(a)(4).

[40] The Public Health Emergency declaration for the Libby Asbestos Site and related information is available on EPA's Region 8 website: http://www.epa.gov/region8/superfund/libby/phe.html.

[41] EPA, "Potential Addition of Vapor Intrusion Component to the Hazard Ranking System," 76 *Federal Register* 5370, January 31, 2011. Information on the status of this effort is available on EPA's Superfund program website: http://www.epa.gov/superfund/sites/npl/hrsaddition.htm.

[42] 40 C.F.R. §300.425(b).

[43] See the "Scope of Response Actions" section of CRS Report R41039, *Comprehensive Environmental Response, Compensation, and Liability Act A Summary of Superfund Cleanup Authorities and Related Provisions of the Act*, by David M. Bearden.

[44] The 2002 guidance and information on the status of revisions to this guidance are available on EPA's Superfund program website: http://www.epa.gov/oswer/vaporintrusion/index.html.

the Superfund program,[45] and to hazardous waste sites addressed under the Resource Conservation and Recovery Act (RCRA), discussed below.

Resource Conservation and Recovery Act (42 U.S.C. 6901 et seq.)

Similar to sites addressed under CERCLA, hazardous waste sites or petroleum sites to which RCRA applies may present risks of exposure to occupants in homes or buildings if water supplies become contaminated or there is the potential for vapor intrusion through the migration of contamination beneath homes or buildings. Subtitle C of RCRA authorizes "corrective actions" to clean up contamination originating from hazardous waste facilities, and Subtitle I authorizes corrective actions to clean up petroleum contamination caused by leaking underground storage tanks.[46] Although CERCLA does not apply to releases of petroleum,[47] cleanup authorities under CERCLA and Subtitle C of RCRA can overlap. Hazardous substances are defined in CERCLA to include substances that meet the characteristics of hazardous wastes under Subtitle C of RCRA.[48] Considering that both CERCLA and Subtitle C of RCRA may apply to the cleanup of hazardous wastes, EPA has issued guidance that is intended to avoid potential overlap or duplication between the two statutes.[49]

Subtitle C authorizes enforcement actions to require owners or operators of facilities which treat, store, or dispose of hazardous wastes to perform corrective actions to clean up contamination originating from those facilities. However, Subtitle C does not authorize federal funding to ensure the performance of the cleanup if the facility owners or operators cannot pay. Rather, Subtitle C primarily is an enforcement authority to require corrective actions that are necessary to protect human health and the environment at active hazardous waste treatment, storage, or disposal facilities regulated under Subtitle C, whereas CERCLA more broadly authorizes EPA to fund the cleanup of hazardous substances under the Superfund program even if there are no viable responsible parties to pursue. EPA has delegated the implementation of the hazardous waste corrective action authorities of Subtitle C of RCRA to all but eight states, including Alaska, Iowa, Kansas, Maryland, Mississippi, Nebraska, New Jersey, and Pennsylvania.[50] In delegated states, EPA still retains its authority to issue cleanup orders to respond to imminent hazards.[51]

---

[45] See the "Brownfields Properties" section of CRS Report R41039, *Comprehensive Environmental Response, Compensation, and Liability Act A Summary of Superfund Cleanup Authorities and Related Provisions of the Act*, by David M. Bearden.

[46] RCRA is the common reference to the Solid Waste Disposal Act. Subtitle C and Subtitle I actually are part of the Solid Waste Disposal Act. RCRA substantially amended the Solid Waste Disposal Act in 1976 (P.L. 94-580), adding the hazardous waste treatment, storage, and disposal authorities of Subtitle C. The Hazardous and Solid Waste Amendments of 1984 (P.L. 98-616) added corrective action authorities to Subtitle C, and the Superfund Amendments and Reauthorization Act of 1986 (P.L. 99-499) added Subtitle I to the Solid Waste Disposal Act to address petroleum contamination from leaking underground storage tanks.

[47] See the "Petroleum Exclusion" section of CRS Report R41039, *Comprehensive Environmental Response, Compensation, and Liability Act A Summary of Superfund Cleanup Authorities and Related Provisions of the Act*, by David M. Bearden.

[48] 42 U.S.C. §9601(14).

[49] EPA, Office of Enforcement and Compliance Assurance and Office of Solid Waste and Emergency Response, *Coordination between RCRA Corrective Action and Closure and CERCLA Site Activities*, September 24, 1996, available on EPA's website: http://www.epa.gov/superfund/policy/remedy/pdfs/rcracorraction-mem.pdf.

[50] Information on EPA's delegation of corrective action authority to the states is available on EPA's website: http://www.epa.gov/waste/laws-regs/state/index.htm.

[51] 42 U.S.C. §6973.

Subtitle I of RCRA authorizes appropriations from the Leaking Underground Storage Tank (LUST) Trust Fund to oversee and enforce corrective actions conducted by responsible parties, or to pay for corrective actions at petroleum sites and recover the costs from the responsible parties. If the responsible parties cannot be found or cannot pay, LUST Trust Fund appropriations may be used to pay for the corrective actions to ensure the performance of the cleanup, similar to the cleanup of sites without viable parties under the Superfund program. The corrective action and enforcement authorities of Subtitle I generally are carried out by the states under cooperative agreements with EPA, financed with appropriations from the LUST Trust Fund.[52] EPA has compiled various guidelines for evaluating risks from vapor intrusion at petroleum sites to assist states in carrying out these agreements.[53]

Radon Gas and Indoor Air Quality Research Act (42 U.S.C. 7401 note)

The Radon Gas and Indoor Air Quality Research Act was enacted as Title IV of the Superfund Amendments and Reauthorization Act of 1986 (SARA, P.L. 99-499). It directs EPA to establish a research program to

> (1) gather data and information on all aspects of indoor air quality in order to contribute to the understanding of health problems associated with the existence of air pollutants in the indoor environment;
>
> (2) coordinate Federal, State, local, and private research and development efforts relating to the improvement of indoor air quality; and
>
> (3) assess appropriate Federal Government actions to mitigate the environmental and health risks associated with indoor air quality problems.[54]

EPA is required to characterize the extent of the indoor air pollution problem; to disseminate information on indoor air quality and solutions; to establish an advisory committee composed of representatives of federal agencies and another of representatives of states, "the scientific community," industry, and public interest organizations to assist the agency in carrying out its research program; and to report to Congress on implementation plans and activities. EPA also is required to provide to Congress appropriate recommendations.

Section 404 of Title IV specifies that it does not authorize EPA to carry out "any regulatory program or any activity other than research, development, and related reporting, information dissemination, and coordination activities specified in this title."

Safe Drinking Water Act (42 U.S.C. 300f-300j-25)

Title XIV of the Public Health Service Act, also known as the Safe Drinking Water Act (SDWA), directs EPA to regulate contaminants in drinking water to protect public health. Generally,

---

[52] For more information, see CRS Report RS21201, *Leaking Underground Storage Tanks (USTs) Prevention and Cleanup*, by Mary Tiemann.

[53] See EPA's Office of Underground Storage Tanks, Petroleum Vapor Intrusion Compendium, available on EPA's website: http://www.epa.gov/oust/cat/pvi/index.htm.

[54] 42 U.S.C. 7401 note.

regulation of contaminants in drinking water is beyond the scope of this report.[55] However, some of these contaminants, such as benzene, xylene, radon, or trichloroethylene, are volatile and may be released to indoor air, for example during showering. To address risks due to indoor air exposure to such compounds, the EPA has cited its SDWA authority to protect against "any adverse effect on the health of persons."[56] In March 2011, EPA announced that it would attempt to regulate volatile organic compounds (VOCs) in drinking water as a group.[57] In addition, the SDWA specifically authorizes EPA to regulate radon to reduce indoor air levels.[58]

Clean Air Act (42 U.S.C. 7401 et seq.)

The Clean Air Act (CAA) does not appear to authorize any EPA activity to assess or directly control indoor air pollution. Although "... the Clean Air Act confers general responsibility to EPA to protect the public health and welfare from air pollution," according to EPA, "its structure and provisions direct EPA to control air pollution outdoors."[59] The CAA nevertheless improves indoor air indirectly when its programs lower concentrations of air pollution outdoors. For example, by restricting emissions of volatile organic compounds (VOCs) from consumer products or architectural coatings (defined under Section 183(e) to include paints, coatings, and solvents) in order to reduce ozone levels in ambient air,[60] EPA reduces potential sources of indoor air pollution as well. Similarly, EPA regulation of wood stoves, to control releases of particulates to the ambient air, may reduce indoor levels of pollution.[61]

Federal Insecticide, Fungicide, and Rodenticide Act (7 U.S.C. 136-136y)

The Federal Insecticide, Fungicide, and Rodenticide Act (FIFRA) requires EPA to regulate the sale and use of pesticides in the United States through registration and labeling of pesticide products. The sale of any pesticide is prohibited in the United States unless it is registered and labeled. FIFRA directs EPA to restrict usage of pesticides as necessary to prevent unreasonable adverse effects on people and the environment, taking into account the costs and benefits of various pesticide uses. EPA has restricted use of various pesticides intended for indoor use, including chlordane, used to control termites, and mercury, which was used to control mildew. In registering pesticides, EPA routinely takes into account risks due to exposure to pesticides through food, drinking water, and indoor air in residences as well as in agricultural fields.

Atomic Energy Act (42 U.S.C. 2011 et seq.)

Under the Atomic Energy Act, EPA issues generally applicable environmental radiation standards for radioactive nuclides, such as radon. When EPA was formed, this authority was transferred to

---

[55] For more information about this act, see CRS Report RL31243, *Safe Drinking Water Act (SDWA) A Summary of the Act and Its Major Requirements*, by Mary Tiemann.

[56] 42 U.S.C. 300f(1)(B), cited by EPA in its *Report to Congress on Indoor Air Quality*, Vol. II, p. 8-8.

[57] EPA, Regulatory Development and Retrospective Review Tracker, National Primary Drinking Water Regulations: Group Regulation of Carcinogenic Volatile Organic Compound (VOCs), http://yosemite.epa.gov/opei/RuleGate.nsf/byRIN/2040-AF29?opendocument.

[58] 42 U.S.C. 300(g)-1(b)(13)(G)(i).

[59] EPA Report to Congress, Vol. II, p. 8-3 – 8-4.

[60] Ibid.

[61] 40 CFR 60.520.

EPA from the Atomic Energy Commission. According to EPA, "other federal and state organizations must follow these standards when developing requirements for their areas of radiation protection."[62] In addition, EPA received the authority "to develop guidance for federal and state agencies containing recommendations for their use in developing radiation protection requirements" and "to work with states to establish and execute radiation protection programs."[63]

Agency for Toxic Substances and Disease Registry

Section 104(i) of CERCLA established the Agency for Toxic Substances and Disease Registry (ATSDR) within the Department of Health and Human Services to assess potential health risks at each site that EPA has placed on the NPL under the Superfund program.[64] The ATSDR also may assess health risks at other potentially contaminated sites in response to petitions. Similar to the scope of EPA's response authority, the ATSDR may examine indoor risks of exposure to hazardous substances if there is potential for outdoor contamination to migrate indoors, or if there is potential for indoor contamination to migrate outdoors and constitute a release of a hazardous substance into the environment under CERCLA.

The ATSDR assesses potential health risks at individual sites based on the likelihood of human exposure to contamination through all pathways of exposure, including pathways that may result in indoor exposure risks such as contaminated water supplies or vapor intrusion.[65] In 2008, the ATSDR issued specific guidance for the evaluation of indoor health risks from vapor intrusion.[66] The purpose of the ATSDR's public health assessments is two-fold: to inform the public of potential health hazards at a contaminated site, and to aid decision-makers in evaluating what cleanup actions may be warranted to prevent potentially harmful exposure. Although the findings of the ATSDR may be used to inform the selection of cleanup actions, the agency does not have any regulatory or oversight authority to direct cleanup decisions by EPA or the states. As such, the ATSDR's role primarily is informational in nature.[67]

Consumer Product Safety Commission

The Consumer Product Safety Commission (CPSC) may prevent or reduce indoor pollution by controlling certain hazards associated with consumer products. The Consumer Product Safety Act (CPSA, 15 U.S.C. 2051-2084), which established the CPSC in 1972, authorizes the CPSC to set a mandatory standard, ban a product, issue a recall, or issue other sorts of regulations or guidance

---

[62] EPA, Laws and Regulations, "Summary of the Atomic Energy Act," October 6, 2011, http://www.epa.gov/lawsregs/laws/aea.html.

[63] Ibid.

[64] 42 U.S.C. §9604(i). In addition to site-specific assessments, the ATSDR also prepares toxicological profiles of hazardous substances commonly found at NPL sites to identify potential health effects that can result from exposure.

[65] The ATSDR also may perform more targeted "health consultations" that focus just on a specific pathway or a specific health effect. The states may conduct a public health assessment or a health consultation for some sites under cooperative agreements with the ATSDR. Public health assessments and health consultations for individual sites are available on the ATSDR's website: http://www.atsdr.cdc.gov/HAC/PHA/index.asp.

[66] ATSDR, *Evaluating Vapor Intrusion Pathways at Hazardous Waste Sites*, February 2008, available on the ATSDR's website: http://www.atsdr.cdc.gov/document/evaluating_vapor_intrusion.pdf.

[67] For more information on the role of the ATSDR, see the "Agency for Toxic Substances and Disease Registry" section of CRS Report R41039, *Comprehensive Environmental Response, Compensation, and Liability Act A Summary of Superfund Cleanup Authorities and Related Provisions of the Act*, by David M. Bearden.

---

to reduce unreasonable risks of injury.[68] However, the CPSA mandates reliance upon voluntary standards whenever compliance with voluntary standards would eliminate or adequately reduce the risk of injury, and substantial compliance with voluntary standards is likely.[69] Moreover, the CPSC is prevented from regulating if needed corrective action could be taken under the authority of the Occupational Safety and Health Act, Atomic Energy Act, or Clean Air Act.[70] Therefore, the CPSC operates by collaborating with the industries producing consumer products and the consuming public. For example, the CPSC researches and promotes best practices for the industries, producing guidelines for manufacturers, importers, distributors and retailers.[71] According to EPA, many CPSC activities emphasize applied research "to provide the technical basis for the development of voluntary standards and to disseminate information to the public."[72]

The CPSA defines "consumer product" as

> any article, or component part thereof, produced or distributed (i) for sale to a consumer for use in or around a permanent or temporary household or residence, a school, in recreation, or otherwise, or (ii) for the personal use, consumption or enjoyment of a consumer in or around a permanent or temporary household or residence, a school, in recreation, or otherwise....[73]

Not all products that might be considered consumer products under the general definition are subject to consumer product safety laws administered and enforced by the CPSC. For example, there are express exemptions for products covered under other statutes, such as tobacco, pesticides, firearms and ammunition, aircraft, boats, drugs, and any article which is not customarily intended for use by a consumer.[74] With specific respect to indoor pollution, entire buildings are not within CPSC authority, and the CPSA does not authorize CPSC to issue indoor air quality or ventilation standards.[75]

CPSC authority to regulate building components is unclear. When CPSC attempted to ban the use of urea-formaldehyde foam insulation under this authority, the regulations were struck down by the courts.[76] In recent years, CPSC has relied on product recalls as well as voluntary methods to reduce consumer risks. For example, CPSC disseminates publications to inform consumers about potential hazards.[77]

The Federal Hazardous Substances Act (FHSA, 15 U.S.C. 1261-1278) authorizes the CPSC to require labeling for household products that are hazardous substances, and bans sale of any

---

[68] See 15 U.S.C. §2056 (2006) (authorizing the Commission to set mandatory standards); 15 U.S.C. §2057 (permitting the Commission to ban products); 15 U.S.C. §2064 (allowing the Commission to require that a manufacturer recall a product).

[69] 15 U.S.C. §2056(b)(1).

[70] 15 U.S.C. §2080(a).

[71] See 15 U.S.C. §2054.

[72] EPA Report to Congress, vol. I, p. 49.

[73] 15 U.S.C. 2052(a)(5).

[74] Ibid.

[75] See ibid. (defining "consumer product" as an article intended to be used at home or school); 15 U.S.C. §2080(a) ("The Commission shall have no authority under this Act to regulate any risk of injury associated with a consumer product if such risk could be eliminated or reduced to a sufficient extent by actions taken under the ... Clean Air Act.").

[76] Gulf S. Insulation v. Consumer Prod. Safety Comm'n, 701 F.2d 1137, 1140 (5th Cir. 1983).

[77] CPSC, Indoor Air Quality Publications , http://www.cpsc.gov/cpscpub/pubs/iaq.html.

children's article that contains a hazardous substance.[78] The FHSA defines "hazardous substances" to include household substances or mixtures that are toxic, corrosive, flammable, combustible, irritants, strong sensitizers, or that generate pressure through decomposition, heat or other means if the substances "may cause substantial personal injury or substantial illness" when used in a foreseeable manner.[79] The FHSA might contribute to the protection of indoor environmental quality, therefore, to the extent that it regulates substances that otherwise might be released through indoor use or storage.

Department of Defense

The Department of Defense (DOD) is authorized to clean up environmental contamination at U.S. military facilities under its jurisdiction and decommissioned U.S. military facilities that were under its jurisdiction at the time the contamination occurred.[80] DOD administers the cleanup of these facilities primarily under its Defense Environmental Restoration Program, subject to oversight by EPA and the states to ensure that applicable requirements are met. CERCLA is the principal federal statutory authority that governs cleanup performed by DOD, but RCRA corrective action also may be used as an applicable requirement at some sites. DOD may address indoor exposure risks in performing the cleanup of environmental contamination at individual sites, but subject to the same scope and limitations as EPA under CERCLA discussed earlier.

DOD's guidance for the implementation of the Defense Environmental Restoration Program generally directs the assessment of all potential pathways of exposure to contamination, including indoor pathways such as water supplies and vapor intrusion.[81] DOD also has developed its own guidelines for evaluating risks from vapor intrusion at sites administered under the Defense Environmental Restoration Program,[82] which may supplement EPA's broader guidance. To augment these efforts, DOD has conducted research under its Strategic Environmental Research and Development program and Environmental Security Technology Certification program to better understand the migration of contamination into homes and buildings through vapor intrusion.[83] This research also could be used to inform the assessment of risks associated with vapor intrusion at sites administered by EPA, other agencies, and the states.

---

[78] See 15 U.S.C. §§1261(p)(1), 1262(b) (2006) (giving the CPSC authority to require labels for household products that are hazardous substances); 15 U.S.C. §§1261(f)(1)(D), 1262(e) (granting the CPSC the authority to ban hazardous substances intended for use by children).

[79] 15 U.S.C. §1261(f)(1)(A).

[80] For more information, see the section on "Cleanup Authorities Specific to Military Facilities" in CRS Report R41039, *Comprehensive Environmental Response, Compensation, and Liability Act A Summary of Superfund Cleanup Authorities and Related Provisions of the Act*, by David M. Bearden.

[81] DOD, *Defense Environmental Restoration Program Management*, 4715 20, March 2012, available on the Defense Technical Information Center website: http://www.dtic.mil/whs/directives/corres/pdf/471520m.pdf.

[82] DOD, *Tri-Services Handbook for the Assessment of the Vapor Intrusion Pathway*, February 2008, available on the DOD Environmental Network and Information Exchange website:

http://www.denix.osd.mil/references/upload/Tri-Serv_VI_Handbook_Final.pdf.

[83] Information on DOD's research of vapor intrusion risks is available on the Strategic Environmental Research and Development program and Environmental Security Technology Certification program joint website: http://www.serdp.org/Featured-Initiatives/Cleanup-Initiatives/Vapor-Intrusion.

Department of Energy

The Department of Energy (DOE) coordinates federal energy policy and energy-related research as required by the Department of Energy Organization Act of 1977 (P.L. 95-91; 42 U.S.C. 7101 et seq.), which created DOE. DOE also implements numerous federal statutes aimed at increasing the efficiency of energy production, transmission, and use, and it investigates the potential impacts of these activities on the environment and human health. The scale and focus of these programs have led to a leadership role for DOE within the federal government with respect to indoor air quality, where DOE is recognized to be an authority on indoor air quality. The Department shares its knowledge with other federal agencies and sometimes assists them with environmental impact statements.[84] It also disseminates information to the general public.

In facilities under its jurisdiction, DOE regulates the use of potentially polluting materials like insulation made with formaldehyde.[85] Other DOE programs focus on mitigating risks from so-called "legacy" contamination which resulted from past activities at facilities that were involved in the production of nuclear weapons or nuclear energy research. DOE's cleanup of these facilities may entail addressing indoor exposure risks. Finally, the Energy Reorganization Act of 1974 ((P.L. 93-438, 42 U.S.C. 5801) specifically authorizes establishment of "programs to utilize research and development performed by other Federal agencies to minimize the adverse environmental effects of energy projects."[86] The three major areas of DOE authority related to indoor environmental quality—energy conservation, cleanup of environmental contamination, and research programs—are discussed in more detail below.[87] DOE also is co-chair of an interagency Committee on Indoor Air Quality, which coordinates research. That activity is discussed in a subsequent section of this report under the heading "Other Federal Agencies and the Interagency Committee on Indoor Air Quality."

Energy Conservation and Production Act (ECPA, 42 U.S.C. 6801 et seq.)

DOE authority to promote energy efficiency in buildings is provided by the Energy Conservation and Production Act (ECPA, 42 U.S.C. 6801 et seq.), as amended by the Energy Policy Act of 1992 (P.L. 102-486), the Energy Policy Act of 2005 (EPAct, P.L. 109-58),[88] the Energy Independence and Security Act of 2007 (EISA, P.L. 110-140), the American Reinvestment and Recovery Act (ARRA, P.L. 111-5), and many other public laws. ECPA authorizes energy efficiency programs targeting residential, commercial, and federal facilities. For example, the DOE Weatherization and Intergovernmental Program provides grants, technical assistance, and information to state and local governments, Indian tribes, "community action agencies," municipal utilities, overseas U.S. territories, and low-income families through programs that use a variety of energy efficiency and renewable energy technologies.[89] These programs aim to retrofit

---

[84] EPA Report to Congress, vol. I, pp. 58-60.

[85] For example, the Bonneville Power Administration requires use of low-formaldehyde materials in residential buildings within its jurisdiction (EPA Report to Congress, vol. II, p. 9-6).

[86] 42 U.S.C. 5820. This authority originally was given to the Energy Research and Development Administration which became the Department of Energy.

[87] EPA Report to Congress, vol. I, p. 57.

[88] For more information about federal programs providing energy efficiency incentives, see CRS Report R40913, *Renewable Energy and Energy Efficiency Incentives A Summary of Federal Programs*, by Lynn J. Cunningham and Beth A. Roberts.

[89] DOE, Weatherization and Intergovernmental Program, October 6, 2011, http://www1.eere.energy.gov/wip/.

existing residences. Although not all of these programs directly affect indoor environmental pollution, they generally strive to avoid undesirable impacts on indoor environments by carefully choosing the materials and methods they employ to reduce energy consumption.

With respect to commercial buildings, ECPA requires the Secretary of Energy to appoint a Director of Commercial High-Performance Green Buildings (Commercial Director).[90] Green building programs generally consider indoor environmental quality. ECPA orders the Director to: (1) establish and manage the Office of Commercial High-Performance Green Buildings; (2) coordinate activities with the General Services Administration (GSA)'s Office of Federal High-Performance Green Buildings; (3) promote research and development of high-performance green buildings; (4) jointly establish with the Federal Director of the GSA office a national high-performance green building clearinghouse to provide high-performance green building information and disseminate research results; and (5) work with GSA and relevant federal agencies to ensure full coordination of high-performance green building information and activities.[91]

ECPA, as amended, specifically directs DOE to "establish, by rule, Federal building energy standards that require in new Federal buildings those energy efficiency measures that are technologically feasible and economically justified."[92] Moreover, the standards must be updated periodically and take into account measures regarding radon and other indoor air pollutants.[93]

Cleanup of Environmental Contamination

DOE has been responsible for the cleanup of over 100 facilities that were involved in the production of nuclear weapons for national defense purposes, and nuclear energy research. Similar to sites addressed under EPA's Superfund program or DOD's Defense Environmental Restoration Program discussed earlier, DOE's cleanup of nuclear facilities may entail addressing the migration of outdoor contamination into homes or buildings via contaminated water supplies or vapor intrusion, or addressing contamination inside a facility to prevent migration into the outdoor environment.

DOE administers the cleanup of these nuclear facilities under its Office of Environmental Management.[94] Although the cleanup of most of these facilities is complete, the cleanup of the larger and more complex facilities is not expected to be complete for several years or decades in some cases. Once the cleanup of a facility is complete, the Office of Legacy Management becomes responsible for the long-term stewardship if the facility no longer would have an ongoing DOE mission.[95] The long-term stewardship of a DOE facility with a continuing mission is administered by the DOE office responsible for that mission.

---

[90] 42 U.S.C. 17081.

[91] Ibid.

[92] 42 U.S.C. 6834(a).

[93] 42 U.S.C. 6834(a)(2)(C).

[94] For more information on the role of the Office of Environmental Management and the status of the cleanup of individual facilities, see DOE's website: http://www.em.doe.gov/Pages/EMHome.aspx.

[95] The Office of Legacy Management also is responsible for the long-term stewardship of sites cleaned up by the Army Corps of Engineers under the Formerly Utilized Sites Remedial Action Program (FUSRAP), which had been transferred from DOE to the Corps in FY1998 for the completion of the cleanup. For more information on the role of the Office of Legacy Management and the long-term stewardship of individual facilities, see DOE's website: (continued...)

CERCLA is the principal federal statute that governs the cleanup of hazardous substances at these facilities. RCRA corrective action authority also governs the cleanup of hazardous wastes generated at these facilities. The Atomic Energy Act primarily governs the management and disposal of radiological wastes and nuclear materials. EPA and the states are responsible for overseeing cleanup actions performed by DOE under CERCLA and RCRA, but there is not a comparable oversight mechanism under the Atomic Energy Act.

DOE Research and Development

DOE has a large research program that investigates means of improving energy efficiency, as well as the sources, presence, and health effects of energy-related pollutants, methods of pollution prevention, and remediation. Originally authorized by the Atomic Energy Act (42 U.S.C. 2011 et seq.) and focused on nuclear power, the research scope broadened with enactment of the Energy Reorganization Act of 1974 (P.L. 93-438, 42 U.S.C. 5801), which terminated the Atomic Energy Commission and created the Energy Research and Development Administration (ERDA; P.L. 93-438).[96] Five DOE laboratories form the National Laboratory Collaborative for Buildings Technologies, including Argonne National Laboratory, Lawrence Berkeley National Laboratory, National Renewable Energy Laboratory, Pacific Northwest National Laboratory, and Oak Ridge National Laboratory.[97] They "work together to advance energy-efficient building technologies," "conduct research and development (R&D), provide technical advice and review DOE plans and activities, and work with ... private sector commercial building owners and operators—to

---

(...continued)

http://www.lm.doe.gov.

[96] Originally authorized by the Atomic Energy Act (42 U.S.C. 2011 et seq.) and focused on nuclear power, the research focus broadened with enactment of the Energy Reorganization Act of 1974 (P.L. 93-438, 42 U.S.C. 5801), which terminated the Atomic Energy Commission and created the Energy Research and Development Administration (ERDA; P.L. 93-438) (DOE, Office of Science, "History," November 21, 2011, http://science.energy.gov/about/history/). That law mandated "... engaging in and supporting environmental, biomedical, physical, and safety research related to the development of energy sources and utilization technologies." The same year, the Federal Nonnuclear Energy Research and Development Act of 1974 (P.L. 93-577) authorized research and development "related to the development and use of energy from fossil, nuclear, solar, geothermal, and other energy sources" and directed consideration of the environmental and social consequences of proposed programs (42 U.S.C. 5813). Three years later, the Department of Energy Organization Act of 1977 (P.L. 95-91) created DOE, and all federal energy-related research (other than research related to the nuclear power industry) was brought under DOE authority. That law aims in part to "assure incorporation of national environmental protection goals in the formulation and implementation of energy programs, and to advance the goals of restoring, protecting, and enhancing environmental quality, and assuring public health and safety" (42 U.S.C. 7112). The Office of Energy Research, now the Office of Science, has responsibility for overseeing basic (as opposed to applied) research conducted by the multipurpose national laboratories (that is, those laboratories not focused on weapons). Many DOE research projects coordinate efforts across DOE laboratories and other public and private entities. For example, DOE has established an Energy Innovation Hub at Penn State University that is focused on developing technologies to make buildings more energy efficient. It brings together researchers from academia, two U.S. National Laboratories and the private sector (DOE, FY2011 Congressional Budget Request, Science, Vol. 4, February 2010, p. 14. Also see an article about the project at http://www.doe.gov/articles/penn-state-lead-philadelphia-based-team-will-pioneer-new-energy-efficient-building-designs.)

[97] DOE, Energy Efficiency and Renewable Energy, Commercial Building Initiative, "National Laboratory Collaborative on Building Technologies," November 21, 2011, http://www1.eere.energy.gov/buildings/commercial_initiative/lab_collaborative.html; DOE, Argonne National Laboratory, "Renewable Energy Research and Development," October 28, 2011, http://www.anl.gov/renewables/research/building_eff.html; DOE, National Renewable Energy Laboratory, "Buildings Research," October 28, 2011, http://www.nrel.gov/buildings/.

---

evaluate and test technologies, establish performance evaluation criteria, and perform energy verification of buildings and systems."[98]

Some projects are of particular interest to indoor environmental quality. For example, the Pacific Northwest National Laboratory, operated by Battelle, develops model building-energy code language.[99] The Environmental and Energy Technologies Division of the Lawrence Berkeley National Laboratory has an indoor and outdoor environmental quality research program that focuses on

- reducing the energy used for thermally conditioning and distributing ventilation air in buildings,

- improving indoor air quality (IAQ), thermal comfort and the health and productivity of building occupants,

- understanding human exposures to environmental pollutants found in indoor and outdoor air,

- improving the scientific understanding of factors and processes affecting air quality, [and]

- developing sound science to inform public policy on the most effective ways of reducing hazardous air pollutants.[100]

At Brookhaven National Laboratory, the Environmental Remediation Science Program (ERSP) seeks to provide the fundamental scientific knowledge needed to address environmental problems that impede the remediation of contaminated sites. ERSP investigates transport of contaminants within the subsurface at DOE sites to better inform long-term site stewardship. Research priorities for the ERSP include defining and understanding the processes that control contaminant fate and transport in the environment and providing opportunities for use, or manipulation of natural processes to alter contaminant mobility.[101] Finally, the Ames Laboratory's Environmental & Protection Sciences Program is conducting research to improve the clean up of hazardous waste.[102] The Pacific Northwest Laboratory also conducts research to improve environmental remediation of hazardous substance contamination. Because many hazardous wastes may migrate indoors, these remediation programs also may be relevant to indoor environmental quality.[103]

---

[98] DOE, Energy Efficiency and Renewable Energy, Commercial Building Initiative, "National Laboratory Collaborative on Building Technologies," July 3, 2012, http://www1.eere.energy.gov/buildings/commercial_initiative/lab_collaborative.html.

[99] DOE, Pacific Northwest National Laboratory, Energy and Environment, Energy Efficiency and Renewable Energy Program, "Building Energy Codes Program" July 3, 2012, http://eere.pnnl.gov/building-technologies/bec.stm.

[100] DOE, Lawrence Berkeley National Laboratory, Environmental Energy Technologies Division, July 3, 2012, http://www.iaqscience.lbl.gov/sfrb.html.

[101] DOE, Brookhaven National Laboratory, "Environmental Sciences Department," July 3, 2012, http://www.bnl.gov/des/.

[102] DOE, The Ames Laboratory, "Scientific Programs," July 3, 2012, http://www.ameslab.gov/research/scientific-programs.

[103] DOE, Pacific Northwest National Laboratory, "Environmental Health and Remediation," July 3, 2012, http://energyenvironment.pnnl.gov/ehr/.

Department of Health and Human Services (HHS)

Health-related programs of the U.S. Department of Health and Human Services (HHS), including those related to indoor environmental quality, are administered by eight agencies in the U.S. Public Health Service (PHS), primarily under the authority of the Public Health Service Act, as amended (42 U.S.C. 201-300mm-61, PHSA). The PHSA directs HHS to conduct and "promote the coordination of, research, investigations, experiments, demonstrations, and studies relating to the causes, diagnosis, treatment, control, and prevention of physical and mental diseases and impairments of man, including water purification, sewage treatment, and pollution of lakes and streams."[104]

The act authorizes grants and information dissemination and mandates an annual report on carcinogens. More specifically, HHS is required to conduct research on the effects of low-level ionizing radiation[105] and, in coordination with other agencies, research on the health effects of pollution originating from "human activity in any place in the indoor or outdoor environment, including places of employment and residences."[106] Various research institutes and centers established under the PHSA, such as the National Institutes of Health (NIH) and the Centers for Disease Control and Prevention (CDC), including the National Institute for Occupational Safety and Health (NIOSH), share this responsibility.

NIH's mission is scientific: "to seek fundamental knowledge about the nature and behavior of living systems and the application of that knowledge to enhance health, lengthen life, and reduce the burdens of illness and disability." To achieve this mission, NIH conducts basic and applied research and disseminates knowledge gained from that research. NIH also trains scientists and develops research tools. Many of the institutes conduct research related to indoor environmental quality, but a few institutes are particularly noteworthy with regard to research relating environmental pollution and health outcomes. The National Institute of Environmental Health Sciences (NIEHS), for example, supports epidemiological studies of relationships between physical and chemical factors and respiratory disease. Similarly, the National Cancer Institute explores factors contributing to the development of cancer, and the National Heart, Lung and Blood Institute has focused on the health effects of parental smoking and other indoor pollutants.

CDC is authorized to educate, assess technology, and conduct epidemiology regarding lead poisoning, asthma, secondary tobacco smoke, and other pollutants (42 U.S.C. 247b-3, b-8, and b-10). Using this authority, CDC proposed for FY2013

> the creation of a Healthy Home and Community Environments program—a new, multi-faceted approach to address healthy homes and community environments through surveillance, partnerships, and implementation and evaluation of science-based interventions to address the health impact of environmental exposures in the home and to reduce the burden of disease through comprehensive asthma control. This integrated approach aims to control asthma and mitigate health hazards in homes and communities such as air pollution, lead poisoning hazards, second-hand smoke, asthma triggers, radon, mold, unsafe drinking water, and the absence of smoke and carbon monoxide detectors. The consolidated program will replace CDC's long-standing National Asthma Control Program and Healthy Homes

---

[104] 42 U.S.C. 241(a).

[105] 42 U.S.C. 241.

[106] 42 U.S.C.242(d)(1).

and Lead Poisoning Prevention Program. CDC will take two years to transition to this new, coordinated approach.[107]

According to CDC, the new Healthy Home and Community Environments program would continue "to collaborate with states and other federal agencies to reduce or eliminate multiple housing-related health hazards," and to support "state and local data collection to be used by HUD and other federal, state, and local agencies to target the most vulnerable populations living in homes with lead-based paint hazards."[108]

Many other statutes authorize specific HHS activities relevant to assessment and control of indoor environmental quality.[109] For example, the Agency for Toxic Substances and Disease Registry (ATSDR, currently within CDC) is required to assess pollution pathways and risks associated with hazardous substances released to the environment at all Superfund and many other contaminated sites.[110] In particular, ATSDR is authorized to investigate the relationship between particular contaminants and disease, and to track the health of people who have been exposed to specific chemical substances.[111]

HHS also has responsibilities under Title IV of TSCA, which mandates a study by CDC and the National Institute for Environmental Health Sciences (NIEHS) to determine the sources of lead exposure to children who have elevated lead levels in their bodies. NIOSH is directed to study ways of reducing occupational exposure to lead during abatement activities and "at a minimum" $10 million was authorized (under P.L. 102-550, Section 1033) to be appropriated for each of the fiscal years 1994 through 1997 for training people who remove or immobilize lead-based paint.

NIOSH obtains its primary authority to conduct research related to indoor environments from Section 20 of the Occupational Safety and Health Act (OSH Act, 16 U.S.C. 651 et seq.). That law established NIOSH to provide scientific support for occupational health and safety regulation. OSHAct empowers NIOSH to investigate work environments at the request of authorized representatives of employees or employers and to develop health-based criteria for toxic substances. Those criteria may then be used by the Occupational Safety and Health Administration (OSHA) to set enforceable safety and health standards. OSHA is discussed below.

Authorities of the Indian Health Service, including those related to indoor environmental quality, are based in the U.S. Constitution and various treaties.[112] Relevant statutes include the Snyder Act of 1921 (25 U.S.C. 13) and the Indian Health Care Improvement Act of 1976 (25 U.S.C. 1601). In addition, numerous other laws, court cases, and Executive Orders define the relationship between

---

[107] CDC, FY 2013 Congressional Justification, p. 198, http://www.cdc.gov/fmo/topic/Budget%20Information/appropriations_budget_form_pdf/FY2013_CDC_CJ_Final.pdf.

[108] Ibid.

[109] Darrel J. Grinstead, Appendix H: Statutory Framework for the Organization and Management of the U.S. Department of Health and Human Services, pp. 209-274, In: Leonard D. Schaeffer, Andrea M. Schultz, and Judith A. Salerno, Editors, Committee on Improving the Organization of the U.S. Department of Health and Human Services (HHS) to Advance the Health of Our Population, Institute of Medicine, 2009, *HHS in the 21ˢᵗ Century Charting a New Course for a Healthier America,* The National Academies Press, Washington, D.C.

[110] ATSDR, "About ATSDR," revised January 1, 2009, visited July 3, 2012, http://www.atsdr.cdc.gov/faq.html.

[111] CERCLA section 104 (i)(6) (42 U.S.C. 9604 (i)(6).

[112] HHS, Indian Health Service, Indian Health Service, IHS Fact Sheets, "Basis for Health Services," April 19, 2012, http://www.ihs.gov/PublicAffairs/IHSBrochure/BasisHlthSvcs.asp.

tribal governments and the federal government. Generally, on tribal lands, the Indian Health Service performs functions similar to those of the U.S. Public Health Service.

General Services Administration

The Federal Property and Administrative Services Act (FPASA), as amended (P.L. 152, codified as amended in scattered sections of 40 U.S.C. and 41 U.S.C.), established the General Services Administration (GSA), transferring to it certain property management functions of other federal entities. Generally, the FPASA authorizes GSA to centralize and oversee federal administrative services, management policy, and provision of products and services.[113] The Public Buildings Act, as amended (40 U.S.C. §3301-3315) specifically authorizes GSA to take certain actions related to property management, for example, to construct, lease, and renovate federal civilian facilities.[114] The Public Buildings Service (PBS) within GSA is the largest provider of office space to federal agencies and is responsible for the design, construction, operation, maintenance, and disposal of thousands of federally owned properties.[115] "PBS owns or leases 9,624 assets, maintains an inventory of more than 370.2 million square feet of workspace for 1.1 million federal employees."[116] PBS establishes design standards and criteria for new buildings, major and minor alterations, and work in historic structures.[117] Environmental standards and guidance are provided by the Environmental Program within PBS to ensure protection of indoor environments in accord with various federal laws and executive orders which apply to all federal agencies.[118] Selected general authorities as well as authorities specific for the GSA are described briefly below.

GSA's actions in the area of energy efficiency closely follow mandates set forth in the Energy Policy Act of 1992 (P.L. 102-486), the Energy Independence and Security Act of 2007 (P.L. 110-140, ESIA) and numerous Executive Orders, most recently President Obama's Executive Order 13514, Federal Leadership In Environmental, Energy, and Economic Performance, and President Bush's Executive Order 13423,[119] Strengthening Federal Environmental, Energy, and Transportation Management. President Obama's Executive Order 13514, Federal Leadership In Environmental, Energy, and Economic Performance, expanded on the energy reduction and environmental performance requirements for federal agencies found in Executive Order 13423.

The Energy Independence and Security Act of 2007 (P.L. 110-140, EISA, codified as 42 U.S.C. 17092) established within GSA an Office of Federal High-Performance Green Buildings. The designated Federal Director of that office is required to coordinate high-performance green

---

[113] U.S. Congress, House of Representatives, Committee on Government Reform and Oversight, Subcommittee on Government Management, Information, and Technology, Hearing, "Federal Property Management and the 50th Anniversary of the Federal Property and Administrative Services Act," testimony of David J. Barram, GSA Administrator, May 4, 1998, http://www.gsa.gov/portal/content/100923.

[114] Other federal agencies have independent statutory authority to construct, maintain, and/or dispose of real property. The Department of Veterans' Affairs, the Postal Service, and Department of Defense, for example, have such authority.

[115] Ibid.

[116] GSA, Public Buildings Service, April 19, 2012, http://www.gsa.gov/portal/content/104444.

[117] GSA, 2003 Facilities Standards (P100), updated April 30, 2010, visited October 13, 2011, http://www.gsa.gov/portal/category/21049.

[118] GSA, "Environment Program Overview," updated November 3, 2011, visited October 14, 2011, http://www.gsa.gov/portal/content/104502.

[119] Executive Order 13423 rescinded several previous executive orders, including 13101, 13123, 13134, 13148, and 13149.

building information and activities within GSA and with other relevant agencies, including DOE. In addition, the Federal Director is to provide to the Secretary of Energy a certification system to encourage a comprehensive and environmentally-sound approach to certification of green buildings. Finally, the EISA mandated cooperation with DOE's Director of Commercial High-Performance Green Buildings to establish a clearinghouse "to carry out public outreach to inform individuals and entities of the information and services [related to high-performance green buildings] available governmentwide" (sec. 423(1)). The Federal Director is required to ensure, "to the maximum extent practicable" that the public clearinghouse "receives and makes available information on the exposure of children to environmental hazards in school facilities" (sec. 503(b)).

President George W. Bush issued Executive Order 13423 in January 2007 making it the policy of the United States that "Federal agencies conduct their environmental, transportation, and energy-related activities under the law in support of their respective missions in an environmentally, economically and fiscally sound, integrated, continuously improving, efficient, and sustainable manner." The order directed federal agencies to implement this policy using specific strategies, including several with potential effects on indoor environments. Those strategies include

- energy efficiency, greenhouse gas emissions avoidance or reduction, and petroleum products use reduction;

- pollution and waste prevention and recycling;

- reduction or elimination of acquisition and use of toxic or hazardous chemicals; and

- high performance construction, lease, operation, and maintenance of buildings.[120]

Congress mandated the use of integrated pest management to reduce pesticide use on federal property when it enacted the Food Quality Protection Act of 1996 amending FIFRA (7 U.S.C. 136r-1). The Code of Federal Regulations (41 CFR 102-74.35) requires reliance on IPM at all agencies subject to GSA authority. Since 1989, GSA has distributed guidance to federal agencies on how to implement IPM.[121]

Although there are no federal regulations for radon specific to the federal government, GSA has adopted EPA guidelines for use in federal buildings.[122]

President William J. Clinton issued an Executive Order 13058, "Protecting Federal Employees and the Public from Exposure to Tobacco Smoke in the Federal Workplace," on August 9, 1997, establishing a smoke-free environment for federal employees and members of the public visiting or using federal facilities. In furtherance of EO13058, GSA issued FMR Amendment 2008-08, which enforces additional restrictions in GSA-controlled buildings.[123]

---

[120] Executive Order 13423, "Strengthening Federal Environmental, Energy, and Transportation Management," January 24, 2007, October 14, 2011, http://www.gsa.gov/portal/content/102452.

[121] GSA, "Integrated Pest Management," October 14, 2011, http://www.gsa.gov/ipm/

[122] GSA, Radon Management, October 13, 2011, http://www.gsa.gov/portal/content/100875.

[123] GSA, Frequently Asked Questions, October 13, 2011, http://www.gsa.gov/portal/content/104203#13.

It is generally GSA policy to enhance indoor environmental quality.[124] To that end, GSA prohibits use of specific pollutants in the construction of its facilities, including

- products containing asbestos;

- products containing urea formaldehyde;

- products containing polychlorinated biphenyls (PCBs);

- products containing chlorinated fluorocarbons;

- solder or flux containing more than 0.2% lead and domestic water pipe or pipe fittings containing more that 8% lead; and

- paint containing more than 0.06% lead.[125]

Department of Housing and Urban Development

The National Housing Act (12 U.S.C. 1701 et seq.) directs the Department of Housing and Urban Development (HUD) to pursue a national goal of providing "a decent home and suitable living environment to every American family" (12 U.S.C. 1701t). Various specific provisions of the act authorize regulatory and voluntary programs affecting the quality of indoor environments. For example, HUD has specific authority under the National Housing Act (12 U.S.C. 1703) and the Manufactured Housing Improvement Act of 2000 (42 U.S.C. 5401 et seq.) to develop minimum construction and safety standards "to assure the livability and durability of" manufactured homes. HUD used this authority to regulate formaldehyde emissions from certain wood products in manufactured homes.[126] In July 2010, when Congress enacted the Formaldehyde Standards for Composite Wood Products Act (P.L. 111-199), it directed the HUD Secretary to update those regulations to ensure that the standards established by TSCA Title VI are implemented.

The National Energy Conservation Policy Act of 1978 authorizes financing for energy conservation improvements in housing[127] "in the form of grants, low-interest-rate loans, interest subsidies, loan guarantees, and such other forms of assistance as the Secretary deems appropriate to carry out the purposes of this section. Assistance may be made available to both owners of dwelling units and tenants occupying such units."[128]

Other statutes authorize HUD activities related to lead-based paint. The Lead-Based Paint Poisoning Prevention Act (LBPPPA, 42 U.S.C. 4822) is the basis for federal regulation of lead-based paint hazards in federally-assisted housing. During the 1970s, the LBPPPA Title II provided grants to cities and communities to develop local programs to eliminate the causes of lead-based paint poisoning. However, funding for poisoning prevention became less available after 1978 when the programs under Title II were combined with other programs into block grants. In 1991,

---

[124] GSA, 1.6 Environmental Policies & Practices, updated April 30, 2010, visited October 13, 2011, http://www.gsa.gov/portal/content/101230.

[125] Ibid.

[126] 24 CFR 3280.308.

[127] HUD, Homes and Communities, "Basic Congressional and Presidential Actions Establishing Major HUD-related Programs," December 5, 2000, October 21, 2011, http://www.hud.gov/basic.cfm. Hereafter HUD Homes and Communities.

[128] 12 U.S.C. 1701z-8.

Congress created the Office of Lead Based Paint Abatement and Poisoning Prevention (42 U.S.C. 3532 note). The Residential Lead-Based Paint Hazard Reduction Act of 1992 (Title X of the Housing and Community Development Act of 1992, P.L. 102-550, which also enacted TSCA Title IV) directs that office to develop a national strategy to eliminate "as far as practicable" lead-based paint (LBP) hazards in all public housing and private housing constructed prior to 1978 that receive federal financial assistance. Title X requires periodic risk assessments and interim measures to reduce identified LBP hazards in such housing. In addition, the law requires inspection for LBP hazards prior to federally funded rehabilitation or renovation. The federal government, acting through HUD, pays for the construction and renovation (including LBP detection and abatement) of public housing, using funds available through the Comprehensive Improvement Assistance Program to carry out the requirements of the LBPPPA, as amended. Title X authorizes federal grants administered by HUD to state and local governments that choose to establish LBP poisoning prevention programs targeted at low-income residents in private housing. Grants may be used to conduct risk assessments and to remove, immobilize, or otherwise reduce the LBP hazard, with particular attention to hazards to children living in housing constructed prior to 1978. For more information about federal lead-based paint programs, see CRS Report RS21688, *Lead-Based Paint Poisoning Prevention: Summary of Federal Mandates and Financial Assistance for Reducing Hazards in Housing*, by Linda-Jo Schierow.

Occupational Safety and Health Administration

The Occupational Safety and Health Act (OSH Act, 16 U.S.C. 651 et seq.) authorizes the Secretary of the Department of Labor, which has delegated authority to the Occupational Safety and Health Administration (OSHA), to issue and enforce health and safety standards to protect employees in office buildings, industrial settings, and commercial establishments. The standards apply to all employers in the private sector and to federal agencies. The OSH Act does not apply to public sector employers at the state or local levels. However, section 18 of the OSH Act gives each state the authority to set its own occupational safety and health standards, by adopting a state plan that provides at least as much protection as provided by OSHA under the OSH Act. Once a state plan is approved by OSHA and is fully operating, employees who work for that state or local government within that state have OSH Act protections. OSHA no longer has jurisdiction in such states. If states adopt plans that only cover public sector workers, OSHA retains jurisdiction over private-sector workers. Roughly half the states have state plans, including four states that protect public sector workers only.[129]

With respect to toxic substances, the act directs the Department of Labor to set "the standard which most adequately assures to the extent feasible, on the basis of the best available evidence, that no employee will suffer material impairment of health or functional capacity even if such employee has regular exposure to the hazard dealt with in such standard for the period of his working life."

To enforce standards, OSHA inspects facilities and may prescribe abatement of any hazards identified or propose civil monetary penalties for violations.

---

[129] Department of Labor, Occupational Safety and Health Administration, "State Occupational Safety and Health Plans," October 4, 2011, http://www.osha.gov/dcsp/osp/index.html.

Office of the Federal Environmental Executive

The Office of the Federal Environmental Executive is authorized by Executive Order 13514 to promote sustainability and environmental stewardship throughout the federal government.[130] Administered by EPA and housed at the President's Council on Environmental Quality, the Office works with the Office of Management and Budget to support sustainability efforts at executive agencies with expertise, detailed guidance, case studies, and tools. It is particularly responsible for ensuring implementation of Executive Orders on federal environmental performance, including those mandating improvements in energy efficiency.

Other Federal Agencies and the Interagency Committee on Indoor Air Quality

Many other federal agencies have statutory authority relevant to the quality of indoor environments. This section briefly describes a sampling of such agencies and their activities.

Department of Transportation

The Department of Transportation (DOT) has responsibility for overseeing indoor environmental quality in "enclosed spaces, such as airliner cabins, buses, and highway tunnels," if these involve interstate commerce.[131] DOT acted through the Surface Transportation Board (formerly the Interstate Commerce Commission) using its very general regulatory authority under the Interstate Commerce Act (49 U.S.C. 13301 et seq.) to prohibit smoking in interstate, commercial motorcoach buses.[132] Through the Federal Aviation Administration (FAA), DOT issued regulations addressing airline cabin air quality for commercial interstate carriers.[133]

Department of Homeland Security

The U.S. Coast Guard (formerly in DOT but currently in the Department of Homeland Security) has jurisdiction over indoor environmental quality of ships in interstate commerce.

Access Board

The Architectural and Transportation Barriers Compliance Board (Access Board) is an independent federal agency devoted to accessibility for people with disabilities. It operates under the authority of the Americans with Disabilities Act (ADA; 42 U.S.C. 12101 et seq.) and the Architectural Barriers Act (ABA; 42 U.S.C. 4151 et seq.) to provide guidelines for construction of accessible buildings. According to the Access Board website,

---

[130] Office of the Federal Environmental Executive, "Federal Leadership in Environmental, Energy, and Economic Performance," October 14, 2011, http://www.ofee.gov/.

[131] EPA Report to Congress, vol. I, p. 75.

[132] 49 CFR Chapter 374 Subpart B.

[133] National Research Council, 2002, *The Airliner Cabin Environment and the Health of Passengers and Crew*, http://www.nap.edu/openbook.php?record_id=10238&page=R1.

ADA standards govern the construction and alteration of places of public accommodation, commercial facilities, and state and local government facilities. The Department of Justice (DOJ) maintains ADA standards that apply to all ADA facilities except transportation facilities, which are subject to similar standards issued by the Department of Transportation (DOT). Federal facilities are covered by standards consistent with those of the ADA issued under a different law, the Architectural Barriers Act (ABA).[134]

Because the Access Board accepts that there are a significant number of people who are particularly sensitive to chemicals and electromagnetic fields, the Board sponsored a study on ways to improve indoor environmental quality. Conducted for the Board by the National Institute of Building Sciences (NIBS), this project brought together various stakeholders to examine building design and construction issues that affect the indoor environment, and to develop an action plan. The resulting report is available on the Access Board website.[135]

Tennessee Valley Authority

The Tennessee Valley Authority is a corporation with a Board of Directors that is authorized to promote the general welfare of people living within its jurisdiction in the valley of the Tennessee River or its tributaries.[136] The Board is authorized to make alterations, modifications, or improvements in existing plants and facilities, and to construct new plants in the area. TVA has investigated indoor radon levels throughout the TVA region and the contribution of radium in building materials. TVA studies also have examined indoor concentrations of volatile organic compounds (VOCs) and nitrogen dioxide. Wood stove design and emissions have been studied, as have indoor pollution levels following weatherization of facilities. TVA distributes information about indoor environmental quality to residents of the region.

Architect of the Capitol

The Act of August 15, 1876 (40 U.S.C. 162–163) directs the Architect of the Capitol (AOC) to maintain, operate, develop, and preserve buildings and land throughout the vicinity of the U.S. Capitol. "This includes the House and Senate office buildings, the U.S. Capitol, Capitol Visitor Center, the Library of Congress buildings, the Supreme Court buildings, the U.S. Botanic Garden, the Capitol Power Plant, and other facilities."[137] The AOC Design Standards address sustainable design, including design to "conserve energy resources, improve environmental performance and increase the use of environmentally preferable products." The AOC's Design Standards change to reflect changes in federal sustainability guidelines and industry standards.[138]

---

[134] Access Board, "ADA Standards Homepage," May 1, 2012, http://www.access-board.gov/ada/.

[135] Access Board, IEQ Indoor Environmental Quality Project, May 1, 2012, http://www.access-board.gov/research/ieq/ ieq_project.pdfhttp://www.access-board.gov/research/ieq/intro.cfm.

[136] 16 U.S.C. 831 et seq.

[137] Architect of the Capitol, About Us/Responsibilities, May 1, 2012, http://www.aoc.gov/aoc/responsibilities/ index.cfm.

[138] AOC, "Sustainability/Overview," May 1, 2012, http://www.aoc.gov/aoc/Sustainability-Initiatives.cfm.

Department of Commerce

The Department of Commerce also has a role in controlling indoor environmental quality, particularly through the National Institute of Standards and Technology (NIST). NIST is a non-regulatory federal agency that promotes "U.S. innovation and industrial competitiveness by advancing measurement science, standards, and technology in ways that enhance economic security and improve our quality of life."[139] NIST research lays a foundation for assessment and remediation of most indoor contaminants. For example, NIST has developed tools and metrics to evaluate the air quality impacts of technologies used in low-energy buildings. In addition, NIST is developing tools to measure the release, distribution, and chemical forms of nanoparticles in a "typical dwelling" that may be emitted by gas and electric stoves, hair dryers, power tools, and candles.[140] NIST staff routinely are involved in the development of standard measurements and procedures as they serve on committees of ASTM International (ASTM), the American Society of Heating, Refrigerating and Air-Conditioning Engineers, Inc. (ASHRAE), the American Society of Mechanical Engineers (ASME), the American Society of Civil Engineers (ASCE), the American Concrete Institute (ACI), the American Institute of Steel Construction (AISC), the National Fire Protection Association (NFPA), Underwriters Laboratories, Inc.(UL), the Society of Fire Protection Engineers (SFPE), the International Organization for Standardization (ISO), the International Council for Research and Innovation in Building and Construction (CIB), the International Code Council (ICC), the Construction Industry Institute, and others.[141] More information about NIST's role is available through its Pollution/Indoor Air Quality portal at http://www.nist.gov/pollution-portal.cfm.

Department of Agriculture

The Department of Agriculture (USDA) through its Rural Development division is "committed to helping improve the economy and quality of life in rural America," as authorized section 2204 of Title 7 of the U.S. Code.[142] For example, the Rural Energy for America Program provides assistance to agricultural producers and rural small businesses to install and maintain renewable energy systems, energy efficiency improvements, renewable energy development, energy audits, and feasibility studies.[143] In addition, Rural Development has adopted into its regulations certain portions of EPA and HUD rules regarding lead-based paint hazard reduction.[144] Similarly, asbestos and radon control measures are adopted from EPA standards. USDA provides Rural Housing Repair and Rehabilitation Loans to "very low-income rural residents who own and occupy a dwelling in need of repairs. Funds are available for repairs to improve or modernize a home, or to remove health and safety hazards."[145] In addition, the Agricultural Research Service

---

[139] NIST, General Information, May 1, 2012, http://www.nist.gov/public_affairs/general_information.cfm.

[140] NIST, "Elusive Ultrafine Indoor Air Contaminants Yield to NIST Analysis," *NIST Tech Beat*, December 6, 2011, May 1, 2012.

[141] NIST, Engineering Laboratory, "Standards and Technical Activities," May 1, 2012, http://www.nist.gov/el/bfrlstandards.cfm.

[142] USDA, "About RD," May 2, 2012, http://www.rurdev.usda.gov/AboutRD.html.

[143] USDA, Energy, "The Rural Energy for America Program (REAP)," May 2, 2012, http://www.rurdev.usda.gov/BCP_Reap.html.

[144] USDA, Rural Development, "Rural Development Housing & Community Facilities Programs," May 2, 2012, http://www.rurdev.usda.gov/rhs/pss/lead_based_paint_information.htm.

[145] USDA, "USDA Rural Housing Repair and Rehab Loans," May 2, 2012, http://www.neighborhoodlink.com/article/Homeowner/Rural_Repair_Loans.

investigates means of reducing indoor contaminant levels both in residences and in facilities where food is processed and stored.[146]

Committee on Indoor Air Quality

Twenty-three federal agencies, including all of those discussed above, are members of an interagency committee that meets at least quarterly to discuss their activities related to indoor air. The Committee on Indoor Air Quality (CIAQ) was formally established in response to the Radon Gas and Indoor Air Quality Research Act (discussed above). That act directed EPA to carry out and coordinate indoor air research and related activities with the assistance of a federal interagency committee and an advisory committee comprised of representatives of the states, "scientific community, industry, and public interest organizations."[147] The current interagency committee has five co-chairs, EPA, DOE, OSHA, NIOSH, and CPSC.[148]

Agencies cooperating in the CIAQ that have not been discussed above include the Department of Interior, National Aeronautics and Space Administration, Small Business Administration, the Department of State, and the Department of the Treasury. These departments and administrations may use their general administrative authority to: improve environmental quality in their own facilities or for facilities they construct or support; implement guidance or regulations issued by EPA or OSHA; or conduct research relevant to their general missions.[149] For example, the National Atmospheric and Space Administration conducts research to determine levels of gases emitted from test materials that might be used in vehicles or stations.[150] The Internal Revenue Service, in the Department of the Treasury, administers the tax code which provides incentives and disincentives to energy conservation and alternative fuels which may affect indoor emissions as well as ventilation rates. For other examples of programs in these agencies, see EPA's 1989 *Report to Congress on Indoor Air Quality*, Volume II: Assessment and Control of Indoor Air Pollution, Exhibit 9-6 on pages 9-9 to 9-10 (EPA Office of Air and Radiation, EPA/400/1-89/001CANR-445).

State and Local Programs

State governments are active and often dominant partners in ensuring safe indoor environments. Many states have statutes relating to radon, asbestos, lead, carbon monoxide, formaldehyde, and

---

[146] USDA, Agricultural Research Service, News and Events, "New Traps 'Bust' Dust—and Indoor Insect Pests," http://www.ars.usda.gov/is/pr/2001/010223.htm.

[147] Precursors to the current committee date back to at least 1979, according to the U.S. General Accounting Office (GAO, now the Governmental Accountability Office), *Indoor Air Pollution An Emerging Health Problem*, CED-80-111, September 24, 1980, p. 14, April 21, 2012, http://www.gao.gov/assets/140/130509.pdf.

[148] The 18 other departments and agencies are: the Access Board (a federal agency committed to accessible design), Department of Agriculture, Office of Architect of the Capitol, Department of Commerce, Department of Defense, GSA, HHS, HUD, Department of Interior, Department of Justice, Department of Labor, National Aeronautics and Space Administration, National Institute of Standards and Technology, Small Business Administration, Department of State, Tennessee Valley Authority, Department of Transportation, and Department of Treasury, as of April 21, 2012, (http://www.epa.gov/iaq/ciaq/members.html.)

[149] For example, see "Current DOD Policies and Directives on Energy Conservation," by Mark Halverson at http://www.wbdg.org/pdfs/usace_ewcdr_dod_policies.pdf, or the U.S. Department of Veterans Affairs' "Green Buildings Action Plan," at http://www.cfm.va.gov/TIL/sustain/GreenBuildMouImplement.pdf.

[150] EPA Report to Congress, vol II, p. 9-9.

other indoor pollutants. Most states have enacted laws prohibiting smoking in workplaces, restaurants, and bars.[151] Some states, such as California, New Jersey, and Washington, have been particularly active in promoting indoor environmental quality to protect worker health.[152] For a list of state and regional radon and indoor air contacts, visit EPA's website "Indoor Air, Where You Live, State and Regional Contact Information."[153] A database of state indoor air quality laws is kept by the Environmental Law Institute.[154] A specialized database focused on schools also is available.[155]

Local governments vary in the scope of authority they are given under their state constitutions, but many forms of local government intervene to promote indoor environmental quality by issuing and enforcing ordinances or issuing and advising citizens about guidance. City zoning, building codes, and licensing of professional contractors can be powerful influences over conditions indoors.

Issues

Numerous agencies have contributed to federal efforts to understand and control indoor environmental quality. Given the diverse nature of pollutants and indoor environments, the number of contributing agencies may not be surprising. However, some analysts have questioned the overall adequacy and efficacy of federal initiatives. Others would prefer a smaller or more focused role for the federal government in addressing indoor pollution, given fiscal limitations or a view that indoor pollution problems might be more amenable to state or local remedies. These issues, the adequacy and efficacy of existing federal actions and the proper role of federal programs relative to state and local programs, are discussed below.

Adequacy and Efficacy of Federal Actions

GAO has been highly critical of federal efforts to address indoor environments. The abstract of a 1980 GAO report on indoor air pollution summarizes its general, continuing view: "Federal efforts to deal with the problem have been piecemeal, receiving little support primarily because no one Federal agency has responsibility for the problem. Until responsibility is assigned to one agency to oversee Federal efforts, they will continue to be ineffectual."[156]

In 1991, GAO looked at the state of indoor air research by the federal government and concluded "... that EPA's emphasis on indoor air pollution, as reflected by the amount of funding for research and related activities, was not commensurate with the health risks posed by the problem

---

[151] American Nonsmokers' Rights Foundation, Summary of 100% Smokefree State Laws and Population Protected by 100% U.S. Smokefree Laws, October 7, 2011, http://www.no-smoke.org/pdf/SummaryUSPopList.pdf.

[152] OSHA, Indoor Air Quality, May 7, 2012, http://www.osha.gov/SLTC/indoorairquality/.

[153] EPA, "Indoor Air, Where You Live, State and Regional Contact Information," May 7, 2012, http://www.epa.gov/iaq/whereyoulive.html.

[154] Environmental Law Institute, Indoor Environments & Green Buildings Policy Resource Center, Database of State Indoor Air Quality Laws, February 2012, May 7, 2012, http://www.eli.org/Buildings/iaq_databases.cfm.

[155] ELI, Database of State Indoor Air Quality Laws: Database Excerpt: IAQ in Schools, February 2012, May 7, 2012, http://www.eli.org/Buildings/iaq_databases.cfm.

[156] GAO, *Indoor Air Pollution An Emerging Health Problem*, CED-80-111, September 24, 1980.

… [and] that better coordination was needed among federal agencies in their indoor air-related activities, including research."[157]

Moreover, GAO reported that "… the indoor air program, unlike other statutorily mandated EPA programs, did not have the kinds of legislatively mandated time frames and goals that tend to drive the resource allocation process and set research funding priorities."[158]

Finally, GAO noted:

> In passing title IV of SARA, the Congress expected EPA to work with other federal agencies that have programs affecting indoor air quality and to develop a national program addressing indoor air pollution. Although CIAQ was established for this purpose, it has not been as effective as it could be because of the limited commitment of other federal agencies. Furthermore, CIAQ lacks a clear charter that establishes the roles and responsibilities of all federal agencies and defines how the agencies will work together to address indoor air issues.[159]

Eight years later, another GAO report was more complimentary:

> notable progress has been made in understanding the problem of indoor pollution and in devising strategies for mitigating pollutant exposures. Consumer products have been reformulated, and building materials and practices have been altered. Guidance documents have also been developed for use by building managers, homeowners, and consumers to help them better understand the causes and sources of indoor pollution and enable them to take steps to prevent pollution problems or remedy them when they occur.[160]

However, GAO also noted that "many gaps in knowledge and understanding of the problem remain."[161]

> The consensus of experts GAO consulted is that significant progress in filling these gaps and resolving these uncertainties will require a comprehensive and coordinated research effort involving multidisciplinary research teams composed of experts in such areas as epidemiology, exposure assessment, medicine, chemistry, microbiology, and building systems.[162]

Experts consulted by GAO also argued that research should promote "a clear understanding of cause and effect relationships—not just documentation of phenomena, as has often been the case up to now."[163]

GAO also has examined more than 90 initiatives of 11 federal agencies aimed at fostering green building in the nonfederal sector.[164] HUD, DOE, and EPA lead more than two-thirds of such

---

[157] GAO, *Indoor Pollution Status of Federal Research Activities*, August 1999, GAO/RCED-99-254, p. 3.

[158] Ibid.

[159] Ibid., p. 6-7.

[160] Ibid., p. 5.

[161] Ibid.

[162] Ibid.

[163] Ibid., p. 9.

[164] GAO, *2012 Annual Report Opportunities to Reduce Duplication, Overlap and Fragmentation, Achieve Savings, and Enhance Revenue*, GAO-12-342SP, February 2012, pp. 175-179.

efforts. DOE chairs an Interagency Energy Management Task Force, which includes 10 of the 11 federal agencies, to encourage collaboration on green building in the *federal* sector.[165] "However, GAO did not identify a governmentwide effort to collaborate on green building issues, including shared goals and common performance measures, for the *nonfederal* sector ..." and concluded that such an effort would be useful to identify opportunities for enhancing efficiency and reducing costs.[166]

Concerns about coordination of federal efforts to address indoor pollution have been expressed by the general public, GAO, and the U.S. Congress in the aftermath of various national crises. For example, after the attack on the World Trade Center, which left surrounding business and residential spaces alike contaminated with asbestos, corrosive dust, and other debris, Congress investigated EPA testing and clean up of the neighborhood[167] and the need for better data collection to assess health impacts.[168] A lawsuit was filed challenging the adequacy of EPA's efforts to test for and clean up contamination.[169] EPA's Inspector General also found the clean-up effort inadequate, and recommended that EPA should "develop protocols for determining how indoor environmental contamination would be handled in the event of a future disaster."[170] The Natural Resources Defense Council issued a report critical of response efforts.

> As a result of the ambiguous jurisdictional setting, some important governmental functions related to the environmental health emergency following September 11th slipped through the cracks. Information on health risks and safety precautions was not effectively communicated to the public. Environmental health protection for workers at Ground Zero was given lower importance compared to other priorities. Residents and office workers were largely left to fend for themselves when confronting questions of debris cleanup and short-term health symptoms that followed from the September 11th attacks. And while several registries are being launched [in 2002] to aid in systematic tracking of health complaints and illnesses of some Ground Zero workers (for example, firefighters), no comprehensive registry of nearby residents, office workers, and students who experienced heath problems related to September 11th was created.[171]

Agencies have coordinated efforts more deliberately since the National Response Plan was released at the end of 2004 specifically for response to national disasters. Nevertheless, after Hurricane Katrina, federal agency coordination regarding the identification and clean up of mold

---

[165] Ibid.

[166] Ibid.

[167] GAO, *World Trade Center EPA's Most Recent Test and Clean Program Raises Concerns That Need to Be Addressed to Better Prepare for Indoor Contamination Following Disasters*, GAO-07-1091, September 2007.

[168] U.S. Congress, Committee Hearing, June 26, 2007

[169] John B. Stephenson, Testimony Before the Subcommittee on Superfund and Environmental Health, Committee on Environment and Public Works, U.S. Senate, *World Trade Center, Preliminary Observations on EPA's Second Program to Address Indoor Contamination*, GAO-07-806T, June 20, 2007, p. 2.

[170] GAO, *World Trade Center EPA's Most Recent Test and Clean Program Raises Concerns That Need to Be Addressed to Better Prepare for Indoor Contamination Following Disasters*, GAO-07-1091, September 2007, p. 3.

[171] Megan D. Nordgrén, Eric A. Goldstein, and Mark A. Izeman, *The Environmental Impacts of the World Trade Center Attacks A Preliminary Assessment*, February 2002, Natural Resources Defense Council, Washington DC, p. 9.

became an issue,[172] as did the formaldehyde levels found in some trailers provided by the Federal Emergency Management Agency and used to house displaced residents of the affected area.[173]

In 2007, GAO examined EPA's continuing efforts to address indoor contamination resulting from the World Trade Center collapse and concluded: "While EPA has acted upon lessons learned following this disaster, some concerns remain about its preparedness to respond to indoor contamination following future disasters. Specifically, EPA has not developed protocols on how and when to collect data to determine the extent of indoor contamination …"[174]

In the future, if climate change increases the frequency or severity of extreme weather events, as some predict, more frequent crises may be expected, sometimes with attendant air quality problems.[175] A report by the National Academy of Sciences warns that many indoor air quality problems might get worse if adaptations to climate change are made without better information and programs aimed at pollution prevention.[176]

Federal, State, and Local Responsibilities

The appropriate role of the federal government in addressing indoor pollution also is open to discussion. In prior Congresses, some policy makers introduced legislation that would have expanded and strengthened federal involvement in achieving indoor air quality; less attention has been given to other aspects of indoor pollution.[177] Other policy makers preferred a more limited federal role.[178] A few have questioned the need for any action, arguing that there was insufficient evidence that a problem existed.[179]

Proposed legislation in the 102nd Congress, H.R. 1066, would have provided "a system for developing a national response plan to be taken to reduce exposure to indoor air contaminants" and would have allowed states "to develop response programs to reduce indoor air pollution" within the states.[180] In addition, H.R. 1066 would have authorized research at OSHA and mandated cooperation among OSHA, EPA, and NIOSH to conduct research and, if necessary, to issue standards.[181] The most recent version of the Indoor Air Quality Act, H.R. 2952 in the 105th Congress, was less ambitious; it would have directed EPA to publish a list of common sources of indoor air health risks and voluntary guidelines for identifying, reducing, and preventing such

---

[172] GAO, *Indoor Mold Better Coordination of Research on Health Effects and More Consistent Guidance Would Improve Federal Efforts*, GAO-08-980, September 2008.

[173] Federal Emergency Management Agency, "FEMA's Ongoing Response to Formaldehyde," February 12, 2008, HQ-08-002b, May 10, 2012, http://www.fema.gov/news/newsrelease.fema?id=42586.

[174] GAO, *World Trade Center EPA's Most Recent Test and Clean Program Raises Concerns That Need to Be Addressed to Better Prepare for Indoor Contamination Following Disasters*, GAO-07-1091, September 2007, Highlights.

[175] Institute of Medicine, 2011, *Climate Change, the Indoor Environment, and Health*, National Academies Press, Washington DC, prepublication copy, p. 5-2.

[176] Institute of Medicine, ibid., pp. 6-15 – 6-16, 8-7 – 8-13.

[177] For example, in the 105th Congress Rep. Joseph P. Kennedy II introduced the Indoor Air Act of 1997, H.R. 2952.

[178] U.S. Congress, House Education and Labor, Health and Safety, *Legislative Hearings on H.R. 1066, the Indoor Air Quality Act of 1991*, 102nd Cong., 1st sess., July 10, 1991, Serial No. 102-41 (Washington: GPO, 1991), p. 127.

[179] Ibid., June 26, 1991, pp. 50-51.

[180] Ibid., July 10, 1991, p. 71.

[181] Ibid.

risks. EPA would have been directed to investigate contractor businesses to determine whether there was a need for a program to certify contractors, and if there was, to establish a voluntary certification program. Finally, the bill would have authorized EPA to provide grants to states and local governments to implement programs to identify, reduce, and prevent indoor air risks. Since 1998, no legislation has been introduced that would comprehensively address federal control of indoor air quality, or indoor environmental quality more generally.

During hearings on H.R. 1066, real estate developers and builders suggested that the federal role should be limited to research for which building owners and developers lack sufficient resources.[182] They argued that building designers and managers already are subjected to building code standards with regional or local application, which they believed would be more effective than national standards, because regional and local standards would be better tailored toward local climates.[183] It is true that local zoning ordinances and state building and housing codes traditionally are used to address many indoor pollution concerns. For example, state and local governments have controlled smoke, dust, carbon monoxide, and pests, simply by requiring adequate ventilation, insulation, screening, filtration, and/or mechanical cooling or heating to improve air quality indoors. State and local regulations also address such problems as lead-based paint, formaldehyde emissions, and pesticide use.

Building developers also noted the active involvement of private consensus organizations, such as the American Society of Heating, Refrigerating, and Air Conditioning Engineers (ASHRAE), as well as real estate trade associations, in addressing concerns about asbestos management and disclosure during real estate transactions.[184] Voluntary standards often are generally applicable, regardless of building use, and they tend to be aimed at preventing rather than remediating problems. By contrast, federal regulations for indoor environments tend to be pollutant or situation-specific, and reactive, addressing cleanup rather than prevention of indoor pollution.

Options

Many options are available to Congress with respect to indoor pollution. Options range from maintenance of the status quo to expansion or reduction of federal involvement in research, information dissemination, financial incentives, or regulation.

Improving on the Status Quo

Some policy makers might prefer to do nothing new, leaving the current statutory directives and authorities described above and associated appropriation levels intact and allowing federal agencies to continue to implement their programs as they have in the past. This approach has the advantages of familiarity and predictability as well as experienced personnel to carry out federal programs. It would entail no new resources. Congress might choose this alternative if it finds that the programs are adequate to address any potential or acknowledged indoor pollution problems.

---

[182] U.S. Congress, House Education and Labor, Health and Safety, *Legislative Hearings on H.R. 1066, the Indoor Air Quality Act of 1991*, 102nd Cong., 1st sess., June 26, 1991, Serial No. 102-41 (Washington: GPO, 1991), p. 124.

[183] Ibid.

[184] Ibid., p. 101.

On the other hand, any inadequacies or inefficiencies in the current system would be expected to persist.

If Congress wants help in understanding whether or not there is a need for current or additional federal programs addressing indoor environments, it might want to form a blue ribbon panel of scientists or stakeholders to examine the state of knowledge about indoor environments and pollutants and how they currently are regulated. A report could form the basis of future oversight hearings and perhaps also legislation.

A third avenue might be to better coordinate current levels of federal involvement, as recommended by the 1997 Presidential and Congressional Commission on Risk Assessment and Risk Management. The Commission recommended legislation that would mandate a coordinated strategy by EPA, CPSC, OSHA, and other federal agencies to address the issue, noting that while outdoor air pollution is extensively regulated, "many problems in offices, public buildings, and homes remain relatively unrecognized and unaddressed."[185] The Commission observed that a more effective and coordinated approach to dealing with this issue was unlikely to emerge without a mandate from the Congress.[186]

Reducing the Federal Role

Alternatively, Congress might conclude that enough already is known about the potential risks of indoor pollutants and that current knowledge justifies reducing federal support for, and conduct of, research and other programs. This option may be appealing if Congress finds that the issue does not merit current efforts or that activities would be better coordinated and conducted by local or state government personnel or by the private sector. The advantages of reduced involvement would be the reduced costs to tax payers, fewer mandates to state and local governments, and possibly reduced distortion of the marketplace for building materials (if such exists), which might be a more efficient guide to consumer preferences for new products and services. Disadvantages might include reduced research and therefore less knowledge as a basis for the design, implementation, and evaluation of agency programs. Depending on where cuts were made, agencies might become less effective at developing or disseminating information, coordinating with other agencies, or regulating indoor environments. Or, to the degree that states, universities, and others may spend more to replace federal efforts, duplicative or inefficient efforts could result in lower cost-effectiveness and possibly a greater use of societal resources. However, if Congress also curtailed federal activities and funding for controlling indoor environments, any inefficiencies due to reduced knowledge might be proportionately less significant.

If Congress ended all federal activities aimed at understanding or controlling indoor environments, any public health impacts of exposure to known (e.g., smoke or carbon monoxide contamination of indoor air) or undiscovered pollutants would remain, or even be exacerbated: Employees and visitors to federal buildings would be exposed to pollutants, and workers might be subject to potentially harmful conditions in commercial establishments if state and local governments did not retain their own programs. The latter result may seem unlikely, given the

---

[185] The Presidential/Congressional Commission on Risk Assessment and Risk Management, *Risk Assessment and Risk Management in Regulatory Decision-Making,* Final Report, Vol. 2, 1997, p. 119.
[186] Ibid.

traditional role of many state and local governments, but indoor environmental controls at the state level are quite variable.[187]

Another path might involve a search for specific federal activities that could be eliminated or reduced. Congress could examine current programs in oversight hearings or ask a panel of experts to inform the process by providing a report to Congress. Legislative action could follow to reduce authority or funding for initiatives that Congress found to be redundant or relatively unimportant. This approach might be able to save money while sacrificing little or no public health benefit.

Increasing the Federal Role

Other possible paths for Congress would involve some commitment to increasing the federal role, perhaps as proposed in H.R. 1066, discussed above. An advantage of an increased federal role might be an increased consistency across states in housing or building codes, or in regulation of consumer products. Interstate consistency could facilitate interstate commerce and reduce some obstacles to business development. Building construction and maintenance might be simplified if guidance and regulations were standardized. On the other hand, increased guidance or regulation might impose a burden on businesses that currently operate in a less regulated environment.

Alternatively, an increased role could be effected simply through budgetary actions, perhaps focused on research and information dissemination initiatives. According to some, federal funding for indoor pollution-related research is disproportionately small relative to the costs that indoor pollution imposes on individuals and society, according to estimates of these costs by EPA and other federal and private sector researchers.[188] Items considered in cost calculations include medical treatment and reduced productivity due to workers' absences when ill and impaired performance on the job due to exposure to indoor pollution. Researchers at DOE's Lawrence Berkeley National Laboratory estimated these costs to the United States in the tens of billions of dollars and productivity gains that might be achieved at a similarly high level.[189]

> For example, nationwide savings and productivity gains from reduced respiratory disease have been estimated at between $6 billion and $19 billion annually. From reduced allergies and asthma, a subset of respiratory diseases, such savings and gains have been estimated at between $1 billion and $4 billion annually. From reductions in the health symptoms that are associated with sick building syndrome, such savings and productivity gains have been estimated at between $10 and $20 billion annually. Finally, from direct improvements in workers' performance that are unrelated to health (because indoor environmental factors can affect comfort and productivity without producing discernible health effects) estimates of productivity gains have been put at between $12 billion and $125 billion annually. According to the DOE scientists, a comparison of the potential economic benefits of improving indoor environments with the costs of achieving such improvements suggests that benefits exceed costs by a very large factor.[190]

---

[187] National Center for Healthy Housing, Training, Housing Codes, June 7, 2012, http://www.nchh.org/Training/HealthyHomesTrainingCenter/TrainingCourses/CodeInspectionforHealthierHomes/StateHousingCodes.aspx.

[188] William J. Fisk and Arthur H. Rosenfeld, Estimates of Improved Productivity and Health From Better Indoor Environments, Indoor Environment Program, Lawrence Berkeley National Laboratory, Office of Energy Efficiency and Renewable Energy, DOE (May 1997). Also published in Indoor Air, Vol. 7 (September 1997) pp. 158-172.

[189] Ibid.

[190] Ibid.

Thus, public health and the national economy might benefit from an increased federal role, particularly if increased funding for research and dissemination prompted states to improve indoor environmental quality. However, there is considerable uncertainty about the effectiveness of expanded federal research and the cost estimates in the referenced analysis.

Author Contact Information

Linda-Jo Schierow
Specialist in Environmental Policy
lschierow@crs.loc.gov, 7-7279

David M. Bearden
Specialist in Environmental Policy
dbearden@crs.loc.gov, 7-2390